Image Worlds

Image Worlds

Corporate Identities at General Electric, 1890–1930

David E. Nye

The MIT Press
Cambridge, Massachusetts
London, England

© 1985 by The Massachusetts Institute of Technology

This book was set in Linotron 202 Baskerville by Achorn Graphic Services and printed and bound by Halliday Lithograph in the United States of America.

Library of Congress Cataloging in Publication Data

Nye, David E., 1946–
 Image worlds.

 Bibliography: p.
 Includes index.
 1. Photography, Industrial—United States.
2. General Electric Company. I. Title.
TR706.N94 1985   778.9′9338762138′0973   85-36
ISBN 0-262-14038-1

For Sarah, Rudy, Danny, and Lisa

Contents

Preface

A decade ago two lectures spurred my first interest in photography. I heard Alan Trachtenberg speak on Lewis Hine and, a few months later, Eugene Smith lectured on his own documentary work. They showed me the importance and the power of photography, and I realized the dearth of work on the subject. At the time I never imagined doing research on it myself, although I began to include an examination of photography in my American studies courses. In 1977 when searching for illustrations for another book, I called General Electric to obtain images of Thomas Edison's early laboratories. George Wise, the company historian, took me to see the General Electric Photographic Archives a week later, and I was astonished to see, in the basement of an old brick building, a room packed with more than 1 million photographs. As I was to learn later from members of the Photography Department, after 1965 the archives had become largely a dead file because at that time the company decentralized, and sales, advertising, and public relations personnel moved to other cities. Although the collection was carefully protected in a vault, it had no full-time curator, and only two or three people knew how to use it.

That afternoon we found several pictures I could use, but in the search I saw many others that stuck in my mind. Images of worker athletic teams, massive electrical turbines, advertising, foreign installations, floods, world's fairs, educational classes, laboratories, and the main streets of U.S. cities. They made an indelible impression, and I was fortunate enough to receive permission to spend many afternoons and evenings pouring over them. I had stumbled on one of the largest collections in the world and wanted to understand it. Only government museums and a few universities have more images than Gen-

eral Electric. Better-known collections such as those at the National Archives, the George Eastman House, and Yale
University contain more carefully selected images, but they
have ceased to be part of their original context as a result of
being gathered in. The corporation's photographs remained in
their original order. As I worked through them from 1892
toward 1965, I began to see patterns emerge that inevitably
would have been lost in any selection of the best images.

I began to understand the evolution of the collection as the
development of a set of photographic categories. Instead of
personal styles, which did not appear, I found repetitions of
formulas that the photographers had used to good effect in
capturing the subjects they were assigned. It was possible to
identify a range of techniques that they consistently employed
and to categorize virtually all of the images. A classification
system that had been based on subject matter when I began
gradually became one based on photographic techniques.

By this time, 1979, I had hired several students to help me
survey the archives systematically, and as we proceeded they
had no difficulty understanding and in some cases refining the
categories. With five people working each week in the collection, company executives renewed their interest in the collection and commissioned me to prepare a catalog of 7,000
representative images, which was published in 1981. Although
this selection had a pragmatic value, since the 1 million images
clearly could not be listed and reproduced, the larger meaning
of the archives was necessarily hidden in such an enterprise. It
would be easy enough to mine such a catalog for photographs
in the conventional categories of social history—women, immigration, urbanization, labor—and publish on each of them,
but the principles of selection in every case would violate the
order I had seen in the archives as a whole. Selection by topic
ignored already existing classifications. And if one did not
understand that primary order, could one reliably impute
meaning or purpose to any of the photographs?

I therefore took the entire archives as my subject. It made no
sense, however, to view the photographs in isolation, as matters
of pure form. I began to examine the company's publications to
see where different images had appeared and to see what sorts
of stories accompanied them. These in turn led me into the
literature of technological history. At the same time I moved in
quite a different direction to understand photography as a

technology and as a means of communication. Thus the research bifurcated, and I began to see the archives in two quite different ways. Corporate and institutional history offered one analytic framework; the literatures on photography, communication, and semiotic theory suggested another. I might have written a book as part of but one of these literatures. In a corporate or technological history the photographs would have served primarily as content. In a semiotic study they would have been forms of communication or structures. Rather than write within either of these established discourses, however, I have placed this book in the gap between them. In doing so I have questioned many contemporary ideas of photography and have viewed the corporation less in terms of the traditional categories of production and consumption than as a powerful communicator.

This is a book about ideology and art, capitalism and photography. The form adequate to contain such a subject was not ready made but custom built. The text is basically historical, telling a story about General Electric that begins in 1890 and ends in the early 1930s. But the shape of the story has not been determined by individual biographies, class conflicts, political developments, or other conventional foci that usually give form to historical narratives. Rather the book is organized according to the emergence of industrial photographic communication and the markets it addressed. The approach should prove more illuminating than conventional, functional analyses of institutions and more accessible than many studies in semiotics.

The year 1930 is more than a mere convenience as the end of this study. The years 1890 through 1930 define a period not only in the company's internal development and in the national economy but in the practice of photography as well. New reproductive technologies emerged in the 1930s changing the photographer's work and the range of possible images. Smaller cameras, new color films, improved color reproduction in magazines, superior flash bulbs, and other improvements collectively transformed the strategies of representation corporations might employ. At the same time business became more conscious of photography with the appearance of *Fortune Magazine* (1929), the popular success of the Farm Security Administration documentary photographers in the mid-1930s, and the appearance of such freelance practitioners as Margaret Bourke-White. Stylistically the depression years also marked a sharp change as futuristic design and streamlining became common in marketing products. The 1930s therefore require a separate book-length treatment as a period when corporate photography became far more self-conscious. The previous forty years witnessed its installation as a social practice, becoming a little noted but central means of suggesting new patterns for the organization of experience.

Acknowledgments

I could not have written this book without help from four institutions. General Electric permitted me to study its Photographic Archives and placed no restrictions on my research. George Wise, company historian, guided me to many sources and saved me from many mistakes. Marty Canfield and Ruth Shoemaker of the Photographic Department oriented me to the archives and helped locate retired staff to be interviewed. Linda Vigars Bailey and Julia Hewitt guided me to sources in the Schenectady company library and introduced me to the Hammond Papers, an invaluable resource. None of their help would have been enough, however, without the support from Chris Anderson, head of photography, and Dave Burke at General Electric, Fairfield, Connecticut, who engaged me to prepare a catalog of the archives covering the years 1890 through 1940. As a result a group of enthusiastic students also spent many hours working in the archives. Without their dedication, humor, and hard work, the catalog that was a precondition for this book could never have been completed. I thank Dana Mintzer, Martha Duval, Michele Beaulieu, Sally Yeates-Battin, Andrew Shore, Jon Titus, Harry Rosen, and Edward Horstmann for their work.

Three institutions assisted greatly in the secondary research and writing. The National Endowment for the Humanities granted me an independent fellowship for American studies research in 1981–1982. Harvard University's Department of the History of Science appointed me a visiting scholar, granting me access to the university's magnificent libraries. I particularly thank Erwin N. Hiebert and Everett I. Mendelsohn for their encouragement. I am equally indebted to the Program in Science, Technology and Society at the Massachusetts Institute of

Technology, which made me a visiting scholar and provided office space and copying privileges. Thanks to Carl Kaysen, director, and his fine staff, my work went more smoothly.

Many other archives and libraries helped me put the General Electric materials in perspective: Schenectady County Public Library; Schenectady Historical Society; New York State Library, Albany; Union College Library; Lynn, Massachusetts, Historical Society; Lynn Public Library; Thomas A. Edison National Historic Site; Edison Institute of the Henry Ford Museum and Greenfield Village, Dearborn, Michigan; Boston Public Library; Harvard University Libraries, particularly that of the Fogg Art Museum; the libraries at MIT; and the Odense University Library.

Portions of this work were first presented as papers. I thank the following organizations and institutions for providing me with a forum and for encouraging me with their interest: the Buffalo Semiotic Circle, Rensselaer Polytechnic Institute, MIT, Harvard University, the University of Massachusetts, University of Vienna, the American Studies Association, the Popular Culture Association, and the Norwegian American Studies Association. Two segments of this work have previously appeared as articles. I thank the *Journal of American Culture* for permission to reprint the first half of chapter 2, and *American Studies in Scandinavia* for releasing the rights to chapter 7.

Many scholars have improved this manuscript through comments and discussion, and I am grateful to them for educating me in their specialties as they pertained to my project: Paul Bouissac, Russel B. Nye, Leo Marx, Janice Radway, John Broomfield, Paul Perron, John Weiss, Martin Krieger, Rosalind Williams, Martin Benjamin, Christen Kold Thomsen, Charles Weiner, and Merritt Roe Smith.

No book ever appears without help from professional secretaries, word processors, and editors. Marianne Jensen, Jill Hansen, and Lis Fischer Nielsen have helped me in many ways during the last two years of this project. No department could ask for better staff. Finally, I thank Sarah Heller and Rudy Heller for word processing, encouragement, and needed distractions, and Danny and Lisa in particular; I hope they will read this book when they grow up.

Image Worlds

1

Introduction

This work examines ideology and art in the specific guise of capitalism and photography between 1890 and 1930.[1] A prior tradition of American studies scholarship has traced the relations of industrialization, politics, literature, and the arts during the nineteenth century. Scholars working in that tradition employed the terms *myth* and *symbol* in their studies of American civilization, producing a synthesis in works such as Henry Nash Smith's *Virgin Land*, R. W. B. Lewis's *The American Adam*, Leo Marx's *The Machine in the Garden*, John William Ward's *Andrew Jackson: Symbol for an Age*, and a host of subsequent studies, including, most notably in recent years, Barbara Novak's *Nature and Culture: American Landscape and Painting*.[2]

Most of the classic works of the American studies movement focused on the middle of the past century. In retrospect it seems clear that they did not provide a model for examining the years that followed. Why not? At the time the school came under attack in the 1960s, the major criticism, which I believe to have been mistaken, was that the myth and symbol approach lacked a clear conception of the relations between economics and politics on the one hand and literature and arts on the other.[3] Many scholars at that time embraced the new social history as an antidote, seeking in its mathematical formulas, oral history, and emphasis on material culture a more complete picture of American society than they believed the older school could offer. Social historians were determined to give voice to the common people of history, focusing on the forgotten mass of humanity who wrote few novels, painted few pictures, and left only traces of its experience in humbler and often only partially preserved form. The new social history emerged at a time of considerable popular unrest, and the ferment lent its energy and conviction.

But the new movement ultimately failed in the same way that it once claimed the older school had failed. It never successfully linked the material and the imaginative, or symbolic, realms of experience. It developed no conception of culture as a whole, believing that assembling many parts was enough. But the parts did not cohere. Instead a range of subdisciplines appeared, each with its own periodization and problems and each increasingly far from the others: women's history, black history, labor history, family history, the history of technology, urban history, immigrant history, and more. The social historians, in short, created no synthesis and had no notion of how to do so. Their myriad case studies exploded many easy generalizations about American cultural uniformity. Their emphasis on the forgotten people of history was a salutary corrective to tendencies in American studies to focus on high culture. And in general their work strengthened our understanding of industrialization, particularly in the century from 1830 to 1930.[4]

Yet social history does not provide a synthesis or a general theory. It does not suggest a way, for example, to understand the large corporations that emerged to dominate American life between 1880 and 1930. It helps us to understand the work force, urbanization, immigration, and many other features of the emerging mass culture, but it does not comprehend the most important institution of that culture. This failing is not accidental but integral to the methodological problem already noted. In its diverse and yet integrated activities, the large corporation simultaneously touches both social history and the myth and symbol school. The size and power of a corporation such as General Electric eclipses that of any other institution except the federal government. It cannot be studied as a whole in a single book. It is not comprehended as several company towns, a managerial team, an educational force, a research and development laboratory, a disseminator of mass consumption goods, a political lobby, a builder of large projects such as the Panama Canal, or a multinational enterprise. Dismembered, General Electric is all these, but to coordinate so many parts and to continue to develop and change, General Electric must be more than the sum of its parts. Once divided into the topics of social history, it cannot be put together again.

To study a large corporation, one must conceive it as a whole rather than as an assemblage of categories developed in studying the family, the immigrant, women, minorities, and cities. This insight first became clear in studying the company's photographic collection. As soon as images of immigrants or of women were detached from the total collection, for example, they lost much of their specific meaning and became illustrations in other kinds of arguments. When seen together, however, the photographs stubbornly acted as a check on any scheme that might carve up the corporation into manageable units, ultimately revealing their organization as a fitting subject in itself. Just as the coordination of a large corporation required the transmission of information and the persuasion of its many employees and constituencies, so too the systematic expression of this ideology in photographs emerged as a key subject.

The photographic collection also suggested a concrete reason why there is such a poverty of work done on large corporations, for here was a mass of artifacts that had been sedulously created and maintained in order to promote positive images of the company. They were not data from third parties or disinterested outsiders. The corporation's creation and control of such materials is a metaphor for its cultural hegemony. The historian confronts an institution bent on controlling the past. Corporations edit archives, control access to papers, underwrite favorable works, destroy evidence (more often through neglect than by design), and lay down a barrage of favorable publicity that tells customers and stockholders how they ought to be understood. A few large companies have established professional archives, notably the Ford Motor Company, but they are exceptions to a general indifference to full study of the most powerful institutions in American society other than in purely economic terms. The only full-length historical study of General Electric was written by a member of its publicity department, John Winthrop Hammond, and published in 1941. It remains the best source for many areas of the company's history.[5] Historians have been content to write only occasional articles about General Electric or have focused on particular aspects of its operations, such as research and development.

Piecemeal studies, no matter how outstanding, cannot give a sense of the corporation as a whole. Instead of social history as it has been practiced, a more holistic approach must be found that takes account of the corporate realities of advertising and public relations, as well as the history of research, labor, management, and sales. The myth and symbol school integrated cultural phenomena with an implicit assumption that each had been created by an individual, whether painter, novelist, poet, or orator. Its practitioners assumed that a pattern could be found in cultural phenomena but were not much concerned with how a message was transmitted or who controlled it. One of the interesting features of Ward's book, for example, was that he could draw on a great many funeral sermons given when Andrew Jackson died, all of which had been composed independently in various parts of the United States. The means of communication then did not permit instant transmission of more than the bare fact of Jackson's death. Ward's argument thereby gains strength because the consistent imagery of those writing and speaking about Jackson came not from a public relations department or wire service but from a set of commonly shared cultural assumptions. A similar study of a twentieth-century figure runs the peril that it may quote from stories manufactured by a publicity department or a news agency. There can be no assumption that a common wellspring of cultural values accounts for similarities in the published responses to events.

Put another way, the corporation's very mode of operation places a structural limit on the method of the myth and symbol school. And since the corporation also challenges the piecemeal practices of the social historians, it is evident that a new methodology is necessary that treats it as a whole rather than as detachable parts and recognizes its role as a symbolmaking, ideological force in American society.

One of the major misconceptions about large corporations is that their form derives from something inherent in technology and the development of capitalism. As a result the existence of corporations is too often taken for granted, as a backdrop. This error is built into the laissez-faire assumptions of American economics teaching and also presumed in traditional Marxist scholarship, in which large corporations are an inevitable development. Recent work in the history of technology has disputed the notion that corporations are inevitable, identical to one another, or even necessary. To take an example germane to this study, Thomas P. Hughes has examined the considerable differences between electrical distribution systems in the United States and Europe.[6] The telephone system in many countries is not a privately operated utility but part of the public sector, with a somewhat different form and social function in different countries. Nothing inherent in the technology of electrification or of the telephone dictates their social use. Monopoly, state control, or many local companies will not necessarily result from the introduction of a new machine.

But when a large corporation does emerge as an end result, as was the case with General Electric, it must develop a sophisticated and complex communication system. Such a system cannot be considered a mere microcosm of the larger society's communications or understood as a simple extension of economic functions. In short it cannot be dismissed as a secondary or tertiary institution but must be studied as the principal instrument coordinating and harmonizing the corporation's activities.

The following chapters thus move from a consideration of one representative corporation's growth to dominance during the late nineteenth century to its consolidation of that position in the first quarter of the twentieth century. The study as a whole treats both management and labor, production and consumption, photographic technique and ideological content. It incorporates many of the findings of social history into a larger pattern that links these disparate spheres together through critical analysis of the company's imagery. These images objectify the corporation's values, presenting in concrete terms its conception of both economic and social relations. Together the corporate photographs express an often contradictory pattern of concerns, visualizing the same subjects in different ways, depending on the audience addressed. Ultimately these contradictions are as important as the specific content of the images themselves. They record the failure of corporations to express a unified vision of the work force, of industrial production, of the manager's role, or of the consumer. In short corporations such as General Electric ultimately failed to conceive a convincing history for themselves beyond the narrow limits of the balance sheet. They did not construct a coherent social reality, even in the imaginary world they visualized.

I

The Sender and the Means of Communication

2

Five Billion Messages: The Creation of General Electric and Its Markets

When the telegraph, the telephone, the electric light first made their respective appearances as commercial utilities, people scarcely knew what to think. That these things could be of vast convenience and daily usefulness to them was an idea which did not immediately dawn upon their minds. They had no conscious desire for any such servants. . . . It was not until people were told, emphatically and repeatedly, what the telegraph, the telephone, and the electric light could do for them, not until they had seen the possibilities of these strange new devices demonstrated before their eyes, that they began to develop a "want."

John W. Hammond
"The Psychology of a Nation's Wants"

Reputation is repetition.

Bruce Barton
Letter to Gerard Swope, president, General Electric[1]

Photographs do not mirror reality; they are social constructions. They are made. General Electric produced more than 1 million different images in the seventy-five years after 1890, addressing a number of distinct audiences through them. This book examines the following questions: What kinds of photographs were made? By whom? When did the company find it important to address each of its audiences? How were the photographs disseminated? And more generally what does corporate photography reveal about the nature of ideology in a capitalist society?

In terms of social impact commercial photography such as that practiced at General Electric can arguably be considered the best-funded and the most influential photography of the twentieth century. It reached audiences of workers, consumers, technicians, managers, and voters with billions of messages each year by the 1920s. These were concentrated in magazines and newspapers, which dominated popular culture before radio and television. Artistic photographs were confined to small circulation magazines and a few museum shows during the same period. General Electric's photographs were consciously tailored to a variety of markets and directed to every family in the United States. They constituted an enormous incursion of private enterprise into the public, symbolic realm, yet they have been little studied. To understand why a company made so many images and for whom, it must first be understood as a business and as a part of history.

Consider the historical atypicality of the economy necessary to produce a General Electric. The economy must be highly industrialized so that it can produce large quantities of iron, steel, copper, glass, porcelain, and other substances. It must be served by an excellent transportation system so that these materials can be delivered to the factory, where skilled workers can work them up to become turbines, generators, transformers, and the like. Large quantities of capital must be available that can be rapidly moved through a sophisticated banking system, which in turn pools the wealth of many individuals. The market must contain many potential customers with the resources to buy General Electric's sophisticated products. The list could be continued; the artificiality of the capitalist marketplace cannot be disputed. Nothing quite like it had existed in 1792 or 1842 in the United States, and no matter how advanced the knowledge of electricity might have been at these earlier dates, a General Electric could not have been created. Such a company could have arisen only at the end of the nineteenth century once the infrastructure of banks, transport, and communications had been established and once an entire generation of workers had come into being with sufficiently complex skills to manufacture its products.

From a more mythic standpoint General Electric was the inevitable outcome of combined scientific and economic developments. These were of equal importance. In terms of the history of science and technology, the company could have been created only after the century of electrical discoveries that began in 1746 with the Leyden jar and concluded with Michael Faraday's studies of electromagnetic induction, which made possible the dynamo in 1831. Between these two dates worked Charles Coulomb, Michael Cavendish, Benjamin Franklin, Luigi Galvani, Alessandro Volta, Humphrey Davy, Andre Ampere, and many others. They left a rich store of observation and theory that would be expanded and systematized in the second half of the nineteenth century. Thomas Edison, Elihu Thomson, and others built on this work to make the inventions later sold by General Electric.[2] Because of its dependence on recent scientific discoveries, such a company differed fundamentally from the iron and steel industry or textiles, whose basic methods had developed over thousands of years and had only been improved by technicians. Cloth had been woven and iron had been forged for centuries; the dynamo, the electric light, and the transformer were new.

Scientific research was a precondition for the emergence of General Electric. It was necessary but not sufficient. Science and invention alone would not have led to an electrical industry, much less the peculiar form of General Electric. The industry itself was possible in only a handful of nations with advanced capitalist societies at the end of the nineteenth century: England, France, Germany, and the United States. The first practical application of the electric light came in the English lighthouses in the 1850s. Twenty years later carbon arc lights were employed to illuminate outdoor sites in Germany and France.[3] By 1878 arc lighting had become a promising business in the United States, with several firms entering the field. Thomas Edison visited one of them in that year.[4] He correctly saw that arc lighting would be used primarily in large public spaces and would prove impractical in homes or other indoor locations. Real growth in the industry awaited the invention of practical, enclosed, incandescent lights. Edison succeeded within two years, largely because he had the backing of J. P. Morgan and several other New York financiers.[5] With their money he was able to employ an extensive staff exclusively for inventive purposes. Edison and his research group were one of the first invention factories, an intermingling of science and investment capital then unique to a few sites in the world. In another society the money might have come from the government, a local community, or a university. That the electrical industry from the start was a private business that had to pay dividends to stockholders is a crucial point. From its inception, profit and the search for new markets were fundamental principles.

Because of its strong financial backing, the U.S. electrical industry grew rapidly, from virtually nothing in 1875 to a $200 million industry in 1900.[6] During this period local capitalists in every major U.S. city collaborated to install electrical generating stations and power lines. Expansion came quickly because the financial institutions in the United States were adequate to fund these installations and because electricity permitted improvement of two already existing consumer services: horse-drawn trolleys and gas lighting. In addition to local capital, large sums were raised to finance the electrical manufacturers themselves, particularly in New York, Boston, and Pittsburgh. Although inventors often complained of insufficient funds, considerable capital was invested before the industry became profitable. And once the many small companies had become profitable in the mid-1880s, the process of consolidation began immediately.

Before the creation of General Electric, a series of mergers in the late 1880s created three giant corporations. The several Edison companies and the Sprague Electric Railway Company merged, incorporating officially in January 1889, to become Edison General Electric.[7] At the same time Westinghouse acquired three small companies: Consolidated Electric Company (1887), the United States Electric Lighting Company (1889–1890), and the Waterhouse Electric and Manufacturing Company (1888). This combination of purchases had "the double purpose of strengthening its position in incandescent lamp patents and adding arc-lighting equipment to its line of products."[8] Not to be outdone, the Thomson-Houston Electric Company of Lynn, Massachusetts, acquired seven competitors between 1888 and 1890 and emerged with the majority of the arc lighting business, a clutch of key patents, and a large pool of skilled personnel.[9] Thus in 1890 there were three large corporations in the electrical industry: Edison General Electric, Westinghouse, and Thomson-Houston. So rapid a transformation of the industry but a decade after its start could have occurred only in a culture where capital had become separated from closely knit family structures and where vast sums could be controlled by a relatively small number of individuals. Control of a company no longer rested in the hands of the workers, the inventors, or the managers at the site but in the hands of stock-holders who had nothing directly to do with the business. To them the closing of many electrical plants did not signify the loss of workers' jobs or the confused movements of workers to new sites. Rather it represented the rationalization of the marketplace, where money alone served as a common denominator. There was nothing natural about such a finance system; it was a profoundly cultural creation, a system of superior abstraction that reduced a tremendous variety of goods and services to a single, flexible network of monetary values.

Nevertheless there were obstructions in that network that could block the rapid movement of capital. In particular patents could exclude a company from an entire market. Even after the many mergers of the late 1880s the patent positions of the three corporations remained extremely confused in many respects. In particular the Thomson-Houston Company held weak patents in incandescent lighting, and Edison General Electric had few patents in the alternating current field.[10] Equally important problems bedeviled the electric street rail-way business, where each had some patents; similar conflicts prevailed through every product line in the industry. Merger promised an end to these potential conflicts; competition virtu-ally ensured many legal expenses and price wars, not to men-tion the possibility of exclusion from new markets. All three competitors considered mergers with each of the other two before the Edison General Electric Company and the Thom-son-Houston Company joined in 1892. They became General Electric. With their merger the entire electrical industry was reduced from fifteen competitors to a duopoly in just five years. Westinghouse and General Electric completed this rationaliza-tion in 1895 by signing a patent sharing agreement, effectively removing the last barrier to market control.[11]

General Electric represented more than a mere monopoly of the marketplace or of patents. Alfred Chandler rightly consid-ered the General Electric merger "more important to the devel-opment of modern industrial management in the United States than were the early trusts" because "General Electric was the first major consolidation of machinery making companies, and so the first between already integrated enterprises. Its products and processes were as technologically advanced and complex as any of that day."[12] Where earlier trusts had been monopolies of raw materials and/or their processing, General Electric excelled in techniques, embodied in its skilled work force, a large body of patents, and talented engineers. Such a dominance based on expertise could be extended into new areas through the development of new products. Properly managed it could become self-perpetuating.

General Electric thus possessed strengths fundamentally new to the marketplace, and it would eventually become a model of stable, virtually unassailed dominance in an industry. Yet in the short run it faced the problems of any other business undergoing a major merger. The Thomson-Houston works produced many of the same products as the Edison factories. After 1892 management decided what products to make at each location. For example, sample light bulbs from both parent companies were tested, and when the Edison product proved superior, the Lynn lamp works was shut down. Management itself consolidated as the entire white-collar staff moved to Schenectady. Thousands of other employees were transferred or laid off. After three years General Electric's work force had shrunk from 10,000 to 6,000.[13]

Not all of these reductions occurred because of the merger, however. The financial depression of the 1890s cut company earnings in half between 1892 and 1895. But even in that bleak year of 1895 the new company had profits of $1.4 million. When the economy recovered, General Electric's size and profits increased rapidly; profits rose to $6 million in 1900 and to $10.8 million in 1910, and they more than quadrupled in the next two decades to $57.5 million in 1930.[14] By then most American homes were electrified; the majority of American industry used electrical power; electric trolley cars criss-crossed American streets; every American city had extensive electric street lights; and new appliances were entering the marketplace every year. The industry that had grown from the fusion of scientific knowledge and capital investment could no longer be understood as a simple function of their combination.

General Electric's growth had become a sustained, self-generating phenomenon. It depended on the creation of new product lines and the discovery of new potential customers. Growth, once based on replacing existing services of lighting and transportation, now required sophisticated advertising and good public relations. As early as 1897 the company had recognized the importance of advertising and publicity, uniting them in a single bureau.[15] In creating the Publicity Bureau executives recognized the crucial importance of disseminating information systematically to reach many different markets. Publicity and advertising also served a wider purpose, counteracting unfavorable public opinion. By 1897 some politicians called for nationalizing the electrical industry;[16] others supported the rights of workers to unionize. Because of its enormous size, General Electric had become far more than an economic entity. While in American law it might be treated as a mere individual, it wielded more power than some small cities. Public relations and carefully crafted advertising were essential to bridge the disparity between General Electric's existence as a giant corporation and its legal definition as a private individual.

In historical perspective, the corporation represents an anomaly. While its activities obviously affect millions of persons, it is largely treated, in law and theory, as if it were simply a private person with private objectives. Thus it can own and manipulate land, fix prices (in effect), and coerce individuals through its control of resources.[17]

The modern corporation affects the entire life of the communities where it establishes its factories and often becomes the sole supporter of families of workers over several generations. Its products have a more widespread effect; they can change the terms of a culture's being in the world. Such a transformation occurred in the case of the electrical industry, which began but a century ago and now underlies every aspect of modern life.

After that industry had been consolidated in the 1890s, it grew rapidly to become one of the ten largest in the United States. And during General Electric's growth to maturity, photography proved to be a fundamental means of communication. The corporation used images to project varying conceptions of the social world to separate groups. To engineers it presented an image of value-free scientific research and technological education; to workers it showed a vision of harmonious, nonunionized social relations. For managers it developed a model of the corporation as a caring family; and for the general public, one of technologically achieved social progress, measured in consumer goods. Using photographs these four visions could be presented as facts rather than as theories. And to these four audiences—engineers, workers, managers, and consumers—General Electric could embody progress in the form most satisfying to each.

These image markets developed out of historical necessity as the corporation expanded over a forty-year period. By 1930 each market had been defined as an audience to be addressed in specific forums—magazines, newspapers, and the like, including more than 900 publications, films, and radio programs. To serve these markets, General Electric each year spent more than $12 million.[18] Additionally it spent an undeterminable amount addressing basic political and economic issues, often covertly, through third parties.[19] All corporate messages addressed audiences for specific purposes that sprang from the nature of the business. That is, both the form and the content of the messages developed directly from the exchange relationship between the company and engineers, workers, managers, consumers, and voters. Because these messages improved the movement of goods and services in the marketplace and simultaneously offered a means to subdivide and define the workplace, they became necessary to the corporation's survival. Contradictions between the messages addressed to each audience in turn measure the inconsistencies of the corporation as it attempted simultaneously to satisfy its engineers, sell its goods, organize the work force, influence the voter, and unify its managers.

The seeming transparency of photographs obscures their ideological function in the corporation's presentation of multiple versions of itself to the world. Each photograph seems prototypically real, a replica of something indisputably actual. Because photographs have this quality, they proved uniquely well suited to the corporation's need to address many audiences, giving its messages the aura of fact. Photography thus proved to be the ideal form of communication in the urban society that grew to dominance between 1890 and 1930.

When the electrical industry began in the 1870s, these developments were unimaginable. Advertising itself was relatively new and remained a sideline of company executives.[20] Public relations as a separate field had not yet been thought of and fell to the individual entrepreneur. Edison provides an excellent example. He adroitly used all the basic methods of both advertising and public relations: spectacular demonstrations, press conferences, parades, window displays, brochures, lectures, and newspaper advertisements.[21] Edison also proved particularly adept at what would become a staple of public relations; he cultivated contacts with the press. This came naturally to an old telegraph operator who had often dealt with newsmen and had once printed a newspaper while working on a train. Thus, in addition to his other inventions, Edison might be called the inventor of public relations.

A good example of this flair for publicity was his campaign against alternating current, which Westinghouse had pioneered. Edison published an article in the *North American Review* illustrating the physical dangers of alternating current;[22] he gave numerous press interviews on the subject; he distributed a booklet outlining his position; he used an outside investigator, Harold Brown, to demonstrate the dangers of alternating current in a public electrocution of a large dog at Columbia University; and he even succeeded in getting New York State to use alternating current in the first trial of the electric chair.[23]

Despite such an onslaught, George Westinghouse was slow to react. . . .Westinghouse at first expected the natural superiority of his system to win in normal competition, but finally he realized that the public, which knew very little about electricity, was being convinced by the Edison attacks. . . . Westinghouse then decided to take another kind of action in his so-called "battle of the currents." He launched his own propaganda campaign.[24]

First, Westinghouse issued his own booklet in response to Edison's. Then he hired a former newspaperman, Ernest H. Heinrichs, as an industrial press agent, in 1889. Heinrichs was the first newspaperman hired by a corporation full time; Alan Raucher considers his appointment to be the beginning of the public relations profession.[25] Significantly, at its inception, advertising was not divorced from public relations but made subordinate to it. Heinrichs paid all the advertising bills, linking the two activities in the minds of his advertising clients.

Like Edison and Heinrichs, most others in the new field had previously worked for the newspapers. They were thus able to place not only advertising but also news releases in the press, using personal contacts with old colleagues and friends. The chief target of public relations of this sort was not the competition but the general public; the chief goal was not promotion of products but promotion of the company itself. No clear line separated advertising and public relations administratively, but the end result of these two activities differed. The advertisement appeared as a company message; the press release did not. The advertisement was paid for; the release was not. Yet to secure such free publicity, large advertising budgets were extremely helpful. The two activities were inextricably intertwined, although the final results appeared separately in the media.

Advertising therefore represented only the visible side of General Electric's publicity work. Its necessity was obvious. But what were the goals of public relations? Raucher explains that "business spokesmen expressed fear that the press—which they called the 'great engine of publicity,'—could crush them. The source of that threat stemmed from widespread criticism of secrecy about corporation finances and operations. . . . Reformers charged that secrecy was detrimental to the public interest."[26] The Public Relations Bureau responded to such critics; it did not operate in a vacuum, sending out positive notices at random. At General Electric it answered progressives who wanted government regulation, labor unions who charged the company with unfair practices, and socialists who called for the liquidation of private utilities. All three groups were strong in the United States at the turn of the century.

In recent years most historians have been persuaded by the arguments of revisionist historians such as Gabriel Kolko and Robert Weibe.[27] They emphasized the destructiveness of competition to large corporations, the disintegration of local and personal ties as the basis for business relations, and the consequent desire within the business community for government regulation. Although these arguments may be persuasive for a large number of American companies, they are not accurate as a description of General Electric, whose activities in these years a company publication explained in 1957.

General Electric succeeded in controlling its market not only through the agreement to share all patents with Westinghouse but also through the establishment of a secret holding company, the National Electric Light Association (NELA).[28] Formed originally in the 1880s, NELA was reformed in 1904, ostensibly as a central organization that would assist small independent electrical companies to compete against General Electric and Westinghouse. It purchased these small companies but left their management intact, offering a range of services, including a scientific testing laboratory, a development laboratory, publicity, and technical assistance. In less than a decade NELA absorbed thirty-seven independent manufacturers, which at times joined of their own volition in order to reap the benefits of a larger association.

None of these companies knew that General Electric owned 75 percent of the stock in NELA, which became in effect a holding company. The corporation retained the right to buy the remaining 25 percent of the stock at any time under an option agreement. Five men held the quarter of the stock outside corporate control, and they directed NELA's operations independently. As a General Electric publication stated a half-century later, "Not a soul outside the five organizers of the National, and officials of the General Electric Company, had the slightest intimation that the latter held a controlling interest."[29] This arrangement made it easier to acquire competing companies and to exercise a growing monopoly power. Simultaneously, then, NELA helped eliminate real competition in the electrical industry while preserving its appearance. The result could not have been better: General Electric did not appear to be a monopoly, and the majority of the profits still came to the company as long as any member of NELA sold the goods.

Under this arrangement it was not necessary to conspire in order to set prices. It sufficed to keep General Electric prices slightly higher and to permit the independents gradually to take on more of the business in bulbs, switches, sockets, and the like. After ten years NELA had greatly expanded its share of the market. "At the outset, the National and General Electric were in a ratio of 20 to 80 as to the respective volumes of production. At the end of ten years, the ratio was pretty close to 50:50."[30] In short General Electric had created the appearance of the kind of competition that Kolko described in *The Triumph of Conservatism* in which many small companies succed in wresting business away from a large monopoly. The holding company preserved the illusion of such competition, and during the decade from 1900 to 1910 General Electric received but little of the criticism leveled at other large corporations such as Standard Oil.

NELA persisted in its covert activities until 1911, when the federal government brought suit against General Electric and thirty-seven others for violation of the Sherman Anti-Trust Act.[31] The company chose not to contest the suit and, avoiding the adverse publicity of a trial, submitted to a judge's decree. The judge ordered that NELA be dissolved. In practice this meant that General Electric exercised its stock option and absorbed the independents. In that sense the government's suit only made explicit a hidden monopoly without breaking it up.

The incident illustrates the complexity of any attempted history of General Electric's advertising and public relations during its early years. Trade name advertising represented only a fraction of its total publicity effort. Even after 1911 NELA continued to exist in name, and its headquarters remained near Cleveland, Ohio, where new buildings were erected.[32] The tie to General Electric had been legally recognized, but it was not publicized. Most Americans did not know that the two were connected, and the sales of NELA products continued to be treated as a separate matter. The products were sold under different trademarks for another twelve years.[33]

Until the 1920s this separation made some sense because NELA and General Electric served somewhat different markets. Most of the NELA companies sold lighting equipment but did not compete in the production of power generating systems. Turbines, generators, transformers, and other large machines were too costly for them to make, while electric light bulbs, plugs, and wiring were comparatively easy to mass produce. Furthermore NELA's markets were concentrated in the Midwest, while General Electric's greatest strength lay in the East. The parent company needed NELA's help in expanding the electrical system in order to increase the demand for heavy electrical machinery. The head of General Electric's International Lighting Division, D. M. Diggs, emphasized the importance of these small manufacturers and of electrical lighting to the growth of the business: "Every branch of the electrical industry owes much to electric lighting, for in all electrical development light is the entering wedge, introducing . . . those many other labor saving devices that increased production and comfort in industry and the home."[34] Once the power lines had entered the home, it became a potential customer not only for light but for electrical power as the motive force in a wide variety of other objects. Electrical lines tied the home to the corporation in a fundamentally new way, prefiguring the intrusion of radio and television. For the first time a continuous and instantaneous link existed between the family and a corporation.

While all the emphasis in advertising and public relations fell on what came into the home as a result, of equal importance was the equivalent flow of money out. As electricity became the energy preferred for almost every domestic necessity, this linkage of the home and the corporation began to appear part of the natural order. It was not. For the first time the spheres of consumption and production were intimately linked by a physical bond. Electrical utilities and manufacturers intentionally strengthened that bond until full electrification appeared to be the equivalent of full civilization. Countless travelers have made this equation in describing remote villages where the people had either no electricity or irregular service. Few have noted that the generation of electricity at one end of the network automatically implies the generation of debt at the other end, creating a reciprocal relationship quite unlike that of the classical market economy.

The electrification of a nation cannot occur as a result of competition in a laissez-faire marketplace. Although such notions might conceivably apply to the production of some other modern goods, such as automobiles, electrification presents quite a different set of problems. A single city can no more have competing electrical systems than it can have competing water supply systems or competing police forces. The possibility that different houses on the same street could be supplied with electricity by as many different companies appeared plausible only briefly in the early twentieth century. Quickly the arguments against any such system became obvious: there were too many duplicated costs in generating capacities, electrical lines, sales personnel, and so on through the entire business. Furthermore varying and unequal demands on the electrical system by users required the exchange of electricity from one neighborhood or town to another. This meant standardized voltages were necessary. Electrification made sense only as a vast, integrated system. Local monopoly and national cooperation were essential if service was to be extended to the maximum number of homes and remain dependable. Laissez-faire made no sense as a description of economic reality for central station operators, any more than the fiction that a corporation was an individual. Here were individuals connected to every home.

The chief issue for central stations after 1900 was no longer competition but how to build the electrical load. Ideally a central station operated most efficiently when it had many customers whose various demands at any given moment averaged out to a constant demand. An exclusively domestic market did not meet this requirement because home owners created demand primarily at night, leaving much of the generating plant virtually idle during the day. After a certain point, therefore, the domestic market could not profitably be expanded unless balanced by other markets with other patterns of electrical use. From the utility's point of view, commercial and industrial customers became essential to the profitability of the whole system.[35]

The stages of the expansion of the electrical system, which in turn shaped the advertising requirements and the photographic work at General Electric, proceeded in several stages. First came the entering wedge of lighting itself, primarily in domestic markets, hotels, and the like. Second came the build-up of a substantial business with industries, street traction companies, and underground railways. These balanced the evening domestic consumption with a heavy demand during the day. Third came the proliferation of home appliances, beginning with fans and heaters before 1910 and gradually expanding to irons, toasters, and electric coffee pots before the tremendous growth in the domestic market after World War I. This expansion included washing machines, refrigerators, stoves, radios, vacuum cleaners, and other large appliances, which together worked a revolution in the American household. The historical order of these three stages could not have been logically reversed. Each built on the previous stage until the market had been fully developed by the middle of the century.[36]

Not surprisingly the marketing strategies appropriate for the early stages were not appropriate for the later stages. At the start the emphasis rested solely on electric lighting and its superiority to gas, and from 1879 until just after 1900 these themes remained central. Thereafter General Electric left expansion of the domestic market more and more to the members of NELA and concentrated on the production of heavy industrial equipment, particularly large motors, transformers, turbines, and hydroelectric machinery, while developing new product lines in electric vehicles, trolleys, and electrical locomotives. To reach potential buyers for these products, the company turned to industrial and business trade periodicals. Until after World War I it paid little attention to domestic goods.

During these same years electrification was encouraged through lowering and manipulating utility rates. Companies established considerable differentials between large and small customers. To build the constant load on a central generating station, they gave large users lower rates than home owners, for example. Utilities found this practice advantageous because their major costs were the fixed expenses of installing and maintaining their generating plant and distribution lines. An idle plant was a dead loss. The more constant the load, the more efficient the operation would be and the lower the rates could go. Lower rates made it easier to attract new customers, spurring yet larger investments in more efficient plants. General Electric benefited from utility expansion because it routinely accepted stock in customer operations as part of the payment for new equipment. It thus became a shareholder throughout the industry as well as the principal supplier of equipment.

Not incidentally Samuel Insull, former chief officer of Edison General Electric, led the industry in the practice of constant rate cutting. Under Insull, "Average rates for all classes of service fell from around 20 cents in 1892 to 10 cents in 1897, to 5 cents in 1906, to 2.5 cents in 1909."[37] Insull's ties with General Electric remained after he left for Chicago to become its energy czar. Not only did he buy quantities of General Electric equipment, but he convinced Charles Coffin, the new president, to develop larger turbines than had ever been built before. Insull put up half the capital for developing these turbines.[38] Later he served as president of NELA when it was still a secret holding company.

Other former Edison men were spread throughout the electrical industry, often in key positions. They were inclined to cooperate with General Electric, NELA, and Samuel Insull, for together they held dominant positions in the highly interdependent industry. Thus the coalition centered on General Electric was reinforced by personal ties among Edison pioneers, previous Thomson-Houston employees, and executives who had moved from General Electric to central stations. The economic network of contractual obligations and stock interests was overlaid by a personal network of friendships and professional associations. This infrastructure of individual contacts, as well as General Electric's market dominance and its extensive advertising in trade journals, ensured the corporation its market position between 1892 and 1920.

During these years the company grew under a variety of names and cultivated the illusion of competition. To the average consumer the electrical industry appeared to be divided into independent sectors, when in fact they interlocked. Local utilities appeared to be autonomous when they were actually partially owned by the large equipment-producing firms, which supplied them in return for both cash and stock. A myriad small companies appeared to battle successfully against Westinghouse and General Electric in the light equipment business, but most of them were part of a hidden holding company. And General Electric and Westinghouse themselves, although they competed, shared patent information for a number of years. From top to bottom the electrical industry was interlaced with contracts, informal ties, and other agreements that ensured the smooth expansion of the distribution system.

After World War I a new situation arose as competitors emerged that sold domestic appliances to be plugged into that same grid. The new market had already begun to develop before the war, but the economies of mass production and distribution came into play only when the majority of the nation's homes had been electrified. At the same time declining utility rates made the appliances more attractive. Before 1920 General Electric made primarily heaters and fans, but other companies entered the field more quickly. Two of the early leaders were the Hughes Electric Company in Chicago and the Hotpoint Electric Company in Ontario, California.[39] Selling electric ranges, heaters, and irons, both companies found a growing market. Rather than compete with them, General Electric bought both in 1919.

That acquisition set a pattern as the company allowed others to pioneer products and then acquired the more successful upstarts. The appliances could then be improved by the research and development arm of the company. These purchases brought a problem with them, however, which had become acute by 1922. Should the General Electric products be marketed separately, or should they all be identified under a single trademark? And should these products be sold through an in-house advertising department or through a professional advertising agency? In short, how much centralization was necessary?

To deal with these problems, the president of General Electric, Gerard Swope, called a meeting of the company's chief officers with appropriate members of the Publicity Department and marketing personnel, on July 25, 1922.[40] The meeting began with a review of current practices. Virtually all of that year's advertising budget of $1,916,000 had been spent on magazines. The opening talk emphasized that the American public bought 10 billion periodicals annually. The advertising department used more than 800 different magazine issues to sell the company's more than thirty product lines. It only occasionally called on outside advertising agencies for help with particular problems. It spent little on newspapers, with the exception of one campaign to sell fans during the summer. But most newspaper advertising came directly from the dealers, who used promotional materials the company supplied to them.

Advertising was only loosely centralized. The dealers worked on their own. This fact, coupled with the use of many different names on the products, obscured General Electric as a major producer for the domestic market. The many brand names had been quite functional in the trustbusting climate of the early part of the century, but, as one official at the meeting remarked, "The General Electric trademark means very little to the average housewife." Or as George Hughes said, with reference to the electric range that still bore his own name, although now a company product: "speaking broadly, the G.E. trademark means nothing."[41] The company even sold electric bulbs under the Mazda trademark, and few knew that they came from General Electric. It sold many appliances under the Hotpoint label with the same result. This multiplication of names seemed mistaken to many in the company's management.

To them the new domestic market suggested a different strategy that identified the corporation directly with its many products, building confidence in the whole line. Yet some officials resisted the idea that all products should be marketed under the company monogram. Their argument ran that if General Electric sells a bad iron, it will hurt the sale of stoves or electric lights. Under this new system a consumer unhappy with one product would stay away from them all. They had another argument as well: wouldn't it be poor business practice to look too much like a monopoly by using a single trademark?

With these issues still unresolved, representatives of three leading advertising agencies made presentations. The most compelling came from Bruce Barton, later nationally known as the author of *The Man Nobody Knows*, a life of Jesus Christ whom he characterized as the greatest salesman in history.[42] Barton's manner was persuasive not only in the book, which became a best-seller, but also in many board rooms. He convinced General Electric's management to unify its product line under a single trademark, arguing that "reputation is repetition."[43] Repeated service, repeated advertising, taken together, would sell any product.

Barton further argued that the preponderance of other businesses did not use in-house advertising, for sound reasons. An outside agency had more expertise and could better understand the market. It had to perform well to survive; the in-house agency did not. Barton insisted that the General Electric monogram appear on every product and in every advertisement. The company thereby emerged as a much larger, visible organization in the mid-1920s after three decades of quiet growth. The change was accentuated because the overall advertising budget increased 600 percent between 1922 and 1930, rising to over $12 million a year.[44]

At the end of the decade one public relations officer reflected on these changes and summarized that "an average of a million dollars a month made it possible to circulate during the year, through newspapers and magazines, more than five billion messages—approximately 200 for every family." General Electric so saturated the media that few could fail to receive constant repetition of its messages. And beyond the printed media, it spent more than $2 million on radio advertising between 1927 and 1931. In this case General Electric sold the medium as well as the message: "Thus General Electric seized upon all types of advertising and has sought to intelligently adapt each individual medium to merchandizing problems which are common to itself, the dealers, the distributors, and the central station companies."[45]

Advertising had proved inseparable from growth and profits, and it usually had a multiplier effect. Sales of electric lights spurred the sale of generators, turbines, and transformers. Sales of trolley cars did the same. Sales of radios not only increased the electrical load but opened a new medium to advertising. General Electric pioneered in the medium, opening powerful stations in Schenectady, New York (WGY), Denver,

Colorado (KOA), and Oakland, California (KGO). Together the three stations reached much of the United States. WGY, for example, reached roughly 3 million people in New England and New York State in 1922 and even more listeners when it became the first station licensed to broadcast at 50,000 watts in 1925.[46]

Yet despite this rapid growth in the radio broadcasting business, General Electric's printed advertising remained central to its sales efforts. There, repeated advertising made the unknown familiar, the exotic a commonplace, the unthinkable a prosaic afterthought. Photography provided an ideal form of repetition, making new products a visual reality as familiar objects inserted into known environments, such as the home or a city street. Photography was not a casual sideline for General Electric but a crucial form of promotion necessary to the company. To a considerable degree, it permitted the customer to visualize change and to possess new products imaginatively.

Photography became a tool that General Electric used to promote fundamental changes in the way Americans lived. Through photographs it sought to reshape the structure of the social world. Yet these changes were continually presented as small conveniences or clear developments from the past, not as revolutionary shifts in the ways Americans illuminated their streets, lived in their homes, traveled, or communicated. Photography helped to smooth these transformations, suggesting landscapes of desires and wants. For the corporation behind these pleasing vistas of new products serving newly discerned wants lay "a broader, more fundamental advertising enterprise which was designed to convince the public of the practicality, the utility and the economy of electricity as a worker for man. This was a fundamental principle. Unless electricity were accepted as household servant, research, engineering, finance, executive planning—these would, in all probability go for naught."[47]

The new domestic market required not only a unified corporate image but also appeals on a human basis. The technical advertising adequate to reach power station engineers would not sell the electric range as a household servant. To make such connections between technology and human service, the intelligent use of photography proved more persuasive than words alone. As Barton presciently observed, "A very successful publisher has a rule that no photograph shall ever be printed in his newspapers unless it contains human beings. You and I are interested most of all in ourselves; next to that we are interested in other people."[48] Photographs automatically created interest when they included other people. Simultaneously they presented an idealized situation as though it were a fact, offering the corporation a powerful medium for persuasion.

By the 1920s General Electric possessed an in-house photographic department that produced more than a million prints a year for a wide variety of uses. In fact that domestic market was the last rather than the first photographic audience defined. While Barton's agency began to administer that segment of the corporation's public relations, there were three other areas that remained strictly under General Electric's control. The first market, or audience, had been perceived at the turn of the century with the growing importance of heavy electrical machinery and long-distance transmission equipment. The company addressed buyers and technicians through trade magazine advertising and its own publication, the *General Electric Review*.[49] The second market, the blue-collar work force, existed within the corporation itself. As these workers became more numerous and potentially more powerful, they also became more difficult to reach. Face-to-face communication on a first-name basis became impossible. At the same time workers were becoming more politically active, and by the end of World War I management believed it necessary to begin publication of *Works News*.[50] The creation of each of these audiences developed directly from the changing market for electrical goods and the transformation of factory production. These audiences were each bound to the corporation in a wide range of economic contracts.

The specialization of work and the growth of a national market thus required specialized ideological strategies. The photographs and accompanying stories varied sharply from publication to publication as every group was encouraged to think only of itself. Stories about or photographs of workers never appeared in the engineer's technical journal; information about new hydroelectric dams or new methods of power transmission did not appear in *Works News*. The horizon of each audience extended little further than itself, while the foreground was filled with images and information of particular interest to it. Segmentation of the corporation into different kinds of work created class lines, which were mirrored in the in-house publications. Separate audiences implied separate ideologies.

The creation of these two publications implicitly called for the initiation of a third magazine addressed to white-collar employees engaged either in sales or middle management. Such a magazine appeared in 1922. Called the *Monogram* and adorned with the company logo, it contained yet a third set of stories and photographs. Finally, a fourth publication, the *Digest*, went to distributors and sales personnel overseas. Each publication defined an audience; collectively they defined General Electric's division of its work force.

In recognizing these divisions, the company became a new kind of corporation. It refused to maintain a single identity— that implied in the legal fiction of the corporation as a private person—and instead multiplied versions of itself. The only commonalities in these shifting identities were a few slogans, a trademark, and two symbolic fathers, Edison and Charles Steinmetz. Except for these abstract constants in the General Electric image, all else varied according to audience. The disintegration of the corporation as a single symbolic entity was required by its simultaneous business in diverse fields. The structure of the marketplace dictated the diffuse and fragmented nature of its presentation of itself to the public and to its employees.

The company's huge photographic file was the only site where the multiple General Electrics existed side by side. Its 1 million images offer visualizations of its products, workers, scientists, executives, and consumers. Taken out of context these photographs seem a strange mélange, which collectively appear to have no order. Only when they are located in the historical development of the company and understood as messages to specific audiences do they make historical sense.

Collectively the archive is far more than evidence of General Electric's interest in and use of photography. It records how a major corporation created ideologies appropriate to different audiences and marketed these constructions of reality through photographs. Corporate images visualized future conditions as though they were already present. They gave the illusion that certain economic and social transformations had already occurred in idealized marketplaces for machinery, labor, expertise, and consumer goods. Furthermore the historical emergence of these markets determined the company's discovery of each audience, beginning with engineers in 1903 and ending with consumers in the 1920s. These markets also circumscribed the possible messages appropriate for each audience.

Although economic conditions determined both message and audience, the specific means of communication, photography, imposed technical restrictions on management even as it offered a new medium of expression. Photographs were more than reactions to market forces. They were first a technology, second a social practice, and only third an art that management could manipulate for its own ends. Before examining particular instances of the use of photographs, therefore, it is essential to understand how they were made and by whom.

Origins, Techniques, and Aesthetics of
Commercial Photography

Commercial photography, in our sense of the term, virtually did not exist between the invention of the daguerreotype and the talbotype (both announced in 1839) and the last decade of the nineteenth century.[1] In these years most photographers were independent entrepreneurs rather than employees of large institutions. A few establishments did produce quantities of carte-de-vistes of famous people, and companies such as E. & H. T. Anthony and Company sold millions of stereographic cards.[2] But in both cases every image produced had to be made directly from a negative. For this reason engravers and draftsmen were employed in advertising and as illustrators for magazines and newspapers before 1890. Corporations generally did not employ a permanent photographic staff before then. When needed, a cameraman could be hired. The Union Pacific Railroad paid A. J. Russell to document the development of their transcontinental line, and he made a number of widely reproduced images, the most famous perhaps being "The Driving of the Golden Spike, Promontory, Utah, May 10, 1869."[3] Other professional photographers, such as Calvin Watkins, William Hunt Jackson, and T. H. O'Sullivan, worked on government survey expeditions in the West during these same years, but in such cases employment was only for the duration of a single project.

Commercial photography as a career came at the end of the nineteenth century due to the confluence of two quite different developments, one commercial and the other technical. First, the large corporations themselves developed after the Civil War. These were the potential employers, each specializing in a line of goods to be sold nationwide. Their factories and products would be the subjects of commercial photography.[4] But to reach a mass audience that read the popular press, photographs themselves were useless because they could not be reproduced directly as part of newspaper and magazine press runs. In order to print a photographic image before 1880, the image had to be transferred from the original negative to a light-sensitive bichromated gelatin film. Then, using the Woodburytype or Albertype processes, this gelatin could be used to produce a surface that took up ink in the shadows but did not do so in the bright areas.[5] The resulting printed images were quite satisfactory as reproductions but cost almost as much as photographic prints and could not be placed in newspapers or magazines unless special papers were used. Both of these photomechanical processes were used almost exclusively in books.

Before photographs could appear in the popular press, a new technical process had to be invented. That process, the halftone, appeared in 1880, permitting a photograph to be printed on the same page with type using ordinary paper.[6] This new technique made possible both photojournalism and commercial photography and gradually replaced other reproductive methods. By 1905 half of all the illustrations in New York City's newspapers were halftones; in the 1920s virtually all new images were.[7]

The impact on magazines was more dramatic. A new kind of mass market magazine appeared in the 1890s, beginning with *McClure's*, which the *Saturday Evening Post, Cosmopolitan,* and *Munsey's* quickly imitated. These newcomers, unlike such staid elders as the *Atlantic Monthly* and *Harper's Weekly*, carried many pages of advertising interspersed with their articles and short stories.[8] And while at first many of these advertisements contained drawings, photographs rapidly began to replace them. The photograph possessed particular virtues as a medium to reach the mass market. Photographs, with their directness and accuracy, seemed to present an object without distortion. They made the unknown product familiar and inserted it in known environments. Consumers could use them to visualize change and possess new products imaginatively.

Corporations began to use photographs in their company magazines in order to explain their operations to important customers and to keep the growing white-collar work force informed of internal developments. These magazines became more common as small-scale capitalism gave way to corporate monopolies. By 1915 the largest corporations, including the Ford Motor Company, U.S. Steel, International Harvester, the Goodyear Rubber Company, and General Electric, had house organs using halftone photography.[9] Census figures record the rapid growth of the photographic profession. In 1880 9,990 persons made their living as photographers; two decades later the number had almost tripled to 27,000. Thereafter the profession grew at roughly the same rate as the rest of the U.S. population.[10] The impact of increasing commercial work more than compensated for the loss of studio patrons with the advent of the Kodak camera.

In the 1880s, however, few companies seem to have required a permanent photographic staff. At first they called on photographic studios to do particular assignments. Later larger firms found it convenient to establish their own departments. The numbers of freelance professionals increased, and in 1908, a magazine, *Able's Photographic Weekly*, began to address the new profession.[11] As revealed in its articles, advertising, and regular reports on photographic meetings, the primary audience was the independent operator. By the early 1920s, however, many of its features were being designed for corporate staff photographers, and in 1926 the editors decided to split their audience and issued another magazine specifically addressed to this group, *Commercial Photographer*.

Able's set the pattern for both magazines. Each had a similar format, emphasizing practical matters in many short notes. Both were larded with advertisements. A typical issue contained twenty-four to thirty pages, of which a third were advertising and a third notes on recent or upcoming meetings of photographic associations. Articles covered lawsuits brought against photographers, the development of photographic companies and their products, and other matters of commercial interest but devoted little space to photographs themselves. The information presented was distinctly practical, featuring articles such as one entitled "Home Portraiture as a Business," which included data on typical fees, advice on how to dress, and the best way to find customers.

Able's also facilitated contact among its readers. Many commercial photographers used its classified advertising section to look for partners, to sell or buy studios, or to advertise for assistants. It thus offers an invaluable guide to the early decades of commercial photography and serves to correct any notion that these photographers lacked professionalism or worked alone in idiosyncratic ways.

The convention programs and reports give a vivid picture of photographers who shared their technical knowledge with one another and strove to reach a high standard as a group. At the New York Convention in 1911, held in the Park Avenue Hotel, members demonstrated methods of posing and offered advice for using the tungsten lights just introduced by General Electric. Two well-known Detroit photographers also gave lengthy demonstrations to show how they worked in the studio. B. J. Falk, "the first photographer in America . . . to bring the Lumière process into commercial use, has consented to give a talk on 'Color Photographs; as made by him in his studio.' " In addition to these four demonstrations, the convention offered two large exhibitions. The more interesting of these undoubtedly was that of 600 prints from fifty-seven German photographers, "from the three great schools of photography . . . supported by the German government."[12] The other exhibition contained members' work, and the best prints received prizes and were then published. The photographers who attended thus could view the best contemporary work by both Germans and Americans in a single place. On the second day of the convention, members could view the New York Metropolitan Museum of Art collection and attend lectures there on composition and form. Such annual meetings offered commercial photographers clear models for emulation and prizes and awards for doing so.

Considered in relation to this overview of commercial photography's emergence in the 1890s and its establishment as a profession by the 1910s, General Electric appears to have developed as the other large corporations did. At its founding in 1892, from the merger of the Edison Electric Company and the Thomson-Houston Company, General Electric established a photographic department at its main plant in Schenectady, New York, and built there a small studio on top of a building. Two images taken in 1893 survive.[13] They show a studio staffed by two men. It had a glass roof at one end to supply adequate light and a darkroom at the other end. The interior was an unencumbered open space. A white sheet stretched on a wooden frame served as the principal backdrop for photographing small machines, some of which sat on the floor beside it. Near the entrance to the darkroom a tripod stood by a window, where a camera could be mounted and aimed directly outside. Thus a large piece of machinery could be hoisted to the roof and isolated outside against the movable white screen. For work farther away from the studio, the photographers could carry a case of glass negatives, like that resting on the floor just below the stairs. All negatives were returned to the darkroom for developing. Later, to make a print, the negative was placed immediately in front of sensitized paper and secured in a wooden frame. It was then exposed to the sun on the small balcony jutting out from one corner on the roof to make an 8 × 10 contact print.

Solar printing continued into the 1920s, although in later years mercury arc lamps also supplied the light. But in the 1890s solar printing on the balcony was sufficient. One of the first photographers, later interviewed by the *Works News*, recalled that in these years, "half a dozen negatives was a big day's production."[14] Often they made only thirty negatives in a month. By the late 1890s, however, production began to increase as photographs were used in more aspects of company publicity. By 1919 the company cameramen had produced and filed 240,000 different photographs, turning them out at a regular rate of 10,000 or more a year after 1900.[15] There is no way to determine how many prints were made from a typical negative, but comparisons with the 1920s suggest an average of one hundred prints each. In 1923 the photographic department made 13,000 negatives and 1.3 million prints.[16]

Clearly the original two or three photographers working on the roof in their small studio of 1893 could not have produced so many images a year without additional staff. The stages of expansion were not recorded, but by the 1920s the staff occupied three floors of a building, employing more than twenty full-time workers, including "Mr. Jones and his assistant . . . four cameramen . . . five . . . engaged in making silver prints, one in making enlargements, while others are engaged in opaquing, framing, making titles, lantern slides, photostats, conducting the clerical work involved, etc."[17]

This staff had come under the control of a company publication bureau in 1897.[18] Soon it had a host of addition functions. Two decades after its founding the bureau published all "the Company's catalogues, bulletins, instruction books, technical reports, agents' handbooks," and two company magazines, the

General Electric Review for engineers and *Works News* for blue-collar workers.[19] The facilities of the Publication Bureau were so extensive that all aspects of a job could be handled there. Once management requested a handbook or magazine story, the photography, writing, layout, and printing could be done in one department, working on a tight timetable. The centralized control also permitted censorship, and the bureau routinely examined "all articles and papers intended for publication which relate to the Company's business or interests." Indeed the bureau even had "a lecture service . . . to give reliable information on the progress of the electrical industry."[20]

To provide these services, the Publication Bureau required 242 full-time employees, and it occupied all of one building and parts of three others. Larger than the faculty of a small university, it created a torrent of photographs, posters, calendars, advertising cards, films, brochures, pamphlets, slides, and releases to the newspapers. In the decade after 1917 more departments would spring up, including an architectural service, three more company magazines, and a powerful radio station, WGY, which for a few years could be heard by one-fifth of the population of the United States.

Photography can therefore be understood as a key element in a powerful ensemble of services at General Electric's command. It was an essential tool the company used to convince audiences and capture markets. Such an expensive department was possible only in a corporation manufacturing a diverse line of products nationwide. The bureau was something fundamentally new in American life, and the public possessed no countervailing force to deal with its massive publicity.

Yet because the photographic department was but one appendage to a large corporate public relations and advertising effort, it received little attention. Only a handful of short articles in the company's own magazines recorded its existence over the years. Had it been part of the federal government, the unit would have been as visible as the famous Farm Security Administration photographers directed by Roy Stryker in the 1930s. Instead the photographers have been almost entirely forgotten. A few still survive. Ralph Carrano, for example, worked in the photographic section for forty-six years, retiring in 1971.[21] In the 1920s he worked primarily as a printer, making between 200 and 400 prints a day. At that time almost all negatives were large, 8 × 10 glass negatives, and he made contact prints from each. The negatives themselves were not always kept, but a print of each was retained and filed in black notebook-sized binders, where they remain today. Printing was still done by sunlight at times, often on the conveniently large windowsills of General Electric's Building Twenty. But more commonly a machine made the prints. Of unusual design, it was built expressly for the company by German mechanics employed at General Electric. Constructed somewhat like a merry-go-round, it allowed the printer to work continuously, feeding in negatives and printing paper and getting prints back after a fixed interval. Printing had thus reached almost an automatic stage by 1920, and visitors to the plant were surprised at the unusual machine and the volume of work the printers could do. One year Carrano and another printer estimated they had made 660,000 prints—more than 50,000 a month. The large volume was possible in part because the company used many prints made on blueprint paper. These were temporary cheap pictures often used in catalogs that would soon be out of date.

Compared to the routine of a printer, the photographers had a more varied life.[22] Their work took them all over the United States. Of the four or five full-time photographers, several would be on the road at any time in the 1920s and 1930s. They always went on specific assignments in connection with a particular campaign, such as the introduction of a new street-lighting system or the installation of a line of products in department stores. In the General Electric plants they photographed new products, the machinery used to produce them, famous visitors, executives, and any other subject required for company publications.

As the number of these publications increased in the 1920s, the kinds of images they needed expanded. The photographers had long since become specialists, leaving others to develop negatives, print, enlarge, and distribute their work. Instead photographers spent much of their time in the field. They made pictures of laundries equipped with General Electric flat irons in Baltimore and Atlanta. They went to the Great Northern Paper Company in Maine and made photographs of the paper pulp mills of Millinocket. They documented the new electrical machinery in the mines of Kentucky and West Virginia, in the shoe factories of Haverhill, Massachusetts, and the Coors Brewery in Colorado.[23] In terms of total number of images made, the majority of the work lay inside General Electric,

but the company also spent comparable funds to permit photographers to visit cities, mines, and mills at a time when U.S.
highways and other means of surface transportation were not
well developed. Pictures such as those from the cotton mills of
South Carolina required days of travel in each direction.

These traveling photographers were professionals. They be-
longed to associations, such as the Professional Photographers
of America, and attended its national and regional conventions, thereby renewing and expanding their acquaintances.
They subscribed to specialized publications and used them to
keep in touch with legal and economic developments in the
profession, as well as the latest photographic technology. Descriptions of other photographic units, published in *Commercial
Photographer* during the mid-1920s, demonstrate that the staff
at General Electric was typical of the profession as a whole.[24]

The Goodyear Factory and General Motors had similar staffs
with the same specialization of work functions and managerial
control of shooting assignments. The kinds of problems they
faced were also quite similar. Cameramen at the General
Motors plants complained that the commercial photographer

is expected by his associates in the factory to produce the desired results under all manner of conditions and circumstances.
Many ideas are conceived by engineers, advertising men and so
on down the line to the maintenance department . . . suggesting
photographs which would never be taken were it necessary to
call an outside photographer. . . . A photograph showing a ten-
thousandth inch clearance in a splined shaft-fitting does not
spell anything to the engineer who wants it. . . . The industrial
photographer is expected to do photomicrography with a commercial outfit, reproduce blue prints with white backgrounds,
reverse Van Dykes and tracings, and give the advertising man a
ten foot bromide while he waits, all of which is received in the
studio as part of the day's work.[25]

In short industrial photographers had to supply not only
prints in quantity but also a wide variety of services. The
Schenectady photographers had to descend into mineshafts to
show electrical equipment in service, go up in planes to take
photographs of factories and other sites, and make night pictures of lighting installations. The considerable problems each
of these situations posed can be readily grasped. Even apparently straightforward images of machines, store windows, and

factory interiors presented special problems, and since such images form the majority of their work, compared to only a few pictures taken in mines or from airplanes, it is useful to understand the complexities that attended making these apparently simple images.

The cameras used at the Schenectady works were large (or full plate) view finder cameras. Since they used 8 × 10 inch plates, they required a long bellows with an extension equal to at least twice the diagonal of the plate. As one expert, George W. Hance, advised, "We must have this focal length that we may obtain good perspective in our machinery and automobile work." The long focus lens distorted far less than a short focus lens or a wide angle lens, Hance continued, providing "more nearly what we are accustomed to seeing with our eyes."[26] For most work, therefore, the bellows would be extended to place the aperture nearly two feet from the back of the camera where the glass plate was inserted. Such a camera could be used only on a tripod, and this in turn had to be heavy enough so that it would not be unbalanced when the photographer moved the bellows forward and back or tipped the entire camera 90° to shoot straight down.

Such large view finder cameras were extremely versatile, despite being cumbersome. If a client needed a view taken from a particular spot or if a wall prevented one from choosing an ideal location, lenses could be changed, the length of the bellows stretched or contracted as need be, and the photograph taken. But to do this the photographer had to know the focal lengths of his lenses, not only individually but also in combination. When in doubt, the photographer could calculate: "A general rule to follow in finding the focal length of a doublet (two elements) when the focal length of each element is known, is to add their lengths and divide by four. So for instance, if we have a front combination of 28 inch and a rear 24 inch we will have (28 + 24/4 = 13) a 13 inch doublet."[27] The shorter the focal length, the greater the angle included; shortening it from 13 inches to 11 1/2, for example, increased the angle of view by 10°. Each such variation required that the distance between the lens and the plate also be adjusted. A good photographer could quickly make both changes as circumstances demanded.

Such equipment was standard throughout the industry and presented the photographer with one further problem. When the proposed shot was viewed through the camera before the picture was taken, the scene was upside down. The formal composition of the image had to be inverted mentally for the photographer to imagine the finished picture. For this reason most photographers also used another camera whose shutter contained "a mirror which reflects the image onto the ground glass at the top of the camera, and a hood above this so that one can look in and see the image right side up." These graflex cameras had come into general use by 1905 and were standard at the Schenectady works.[28]

Familiarity with these cameras and the use of a variety of lenses represented only the beginning. The commercial photographer shared these tools of the trade with any other photographer. What made commercial work different were the subjects. In general the subjects were static and did not require fast work. The commercial photographer captured not action but the fixed qualities of a thing. This restriction encouraged an intense exploration of what could still be varied, particularly the length of exposures and the manipulation of background and light. Paradoxically, however, successful industrial images appear natural and normal although achieved with unusual techniques.

Four examples will suggest the problems industrial subjects presented and the natural appearance of the solutions. First, consider machinery, a photographic subject that would seem straightforward. An anonymous writer in *Wilson's Photographic Magazine* offered a study of ways to take such pictures:

The "pose" of a piece of machinery may seem a strange expression, yet this is a subject which must have very careful attention if the photograph is to show it at its best. Reciprocating parts should not be shown at the end of their travel; their functions and form are much easier seen, as a rule, if they are in some intermediate, but not exactly intermediate, position. Even such a detail as a row of lubricators, or of cocks or switches, looks better if they are all arranged in the same position.[29]

An industrial photographer learned to spend a great deal of time searching for the best angle to shoot from and in doing so did not hesitate to move objects, polish surfaces, or otherwise modify the surroundings. Unlike the documentary or artistic cameraman, who usually refused to intervene in a scene, the industrial photographer controlled as much as possible. Once the machine had been posed, the chief problem was lighting. Since the location was often dark or shadowy, a variety of strategies was common. The wall behind the machine could be whitewashed or covered with newspapers. If the wall were not nearby or could not be adapted to the photographer's needs, then a "banner, made by gumming together a number of newspapers and mounting them on a light framework, is sometimes very useful. It may be carried by a couple of laborers" who were required to keep it moving during the exposure so that it would appear as an undifferentiated light gray background.[30] Even with these precautions to ensure a good background, however, the harsh contrasts provided by daylight could easily ruin a picture so that a night exposure was often preferable. This was particularly true if the camera had to be placed in a doorway or in front of a window because sunlight could be reflected from the lens mount or other pieces of metal in the room, again ruining the exposure. In such cases the industrial photographer preferred "to get all ready by daylight, and then to wait until dark, when the work can be photographed by magnesium."[31] In that case, however, a good deal of magnesium had to be burned in such a way that its light was well diffused through the room rather than casting sharp shadows. One way to achieve this was by putting the magnesium ribbon inside a wooden packing case and covering the front with tissue paper to diffuse the light. The use of such a box was doubly advisable since during a prolonged exposure, magnesium smoke could drift in front of the camera and blur the image. To top off all these precautions and preparations, at times sand might be spread on the floor in a square around the machine to frame it. The resulting photograph, which would appear to be simple, might have cost an entire day's work, counting eight hours from the time the photographer left the studio, set up, waited for nightfall, lit the magnesium, got two workers to begin moving a screen of newspapers around behind the machine to be photographed, and then, finally, unstopped his lens. The exposure itself might take half an hour.[32]

Long exposures were used even in daytime, although here another problem emerged, as George Hance recalled. In one factory, "The engine was unfinished and the vibration throughout the shop was bad, but [he] made use of the noon hour shut down and gave the full hour's exposure."[33] Similar problems must have beset the anonymous General Electric cameraman who had to screen off the boring mill at William Sellers & Company. The white barrier highlighted the machine's details but at the cost of considerable time to construct it. The unnatural evenness of the light suggests other manipulations as well.

As this example amply demonstrates, the appearance of a photograph offers no clue to the way it was obtained. In the 1930s, lighting problems would be alleviated by using General Electric's own Mazda flash bulbs and special high-intensity lamps, but the early images were achieved through virtually forgotten techniques.

A second example illustrates this point. Smaller machines and products usually were shot against a white backdrop such as that shown in the 1893 photograph of the Schenectady studio. These would seem to be much easier photographs to make. Such was not the case. Most of these smaller items were new machines and consumer goods, whose polished and shiny surfaces reflected light. An early domestic range (c. 1918) compounded these difficulties since parts of it, such as the stove top, would appear better if they gleamed. Photographers in such cases could selectively dull surfaces. Here is a typical technique: "An oil paste shoe polish was rubbed on over the pattern, and then wiped off, leaving a little. . . . Then the entire surface was puttied with common putty and then any overlapping of the putty dabs were blended with absorbent cotton. The shoe polish and putty will both come off easily with a little gasoline and a soft brush to get down in the cracks."[34] The success of such a technique hid it from view. The putty was applied only in order to make the surface appear normal in the photograph, and consequently one cannot determine by looking at them in the resulting images if products were doctored in this way.

One can be more certain about the means used to shoot the interiors of buildings, particularly mills and other poorly lighted sites. Rather than increase the light artificially, photographers generally blocked the windows with red flannel, removing it for a few seconds of direct light at the end of an extended exposure. And they had another weapon at their disposal, the nonhalation plate, especially made for indoor work. As George Hance explained, the nonhalation plate was coated with two different emulsions: "By that I mean that next to the glass we have a very slow, thick emulsion, which will prevent the extreme highlights from going through to the glass and reflecting, or bouncing back, giving us what we commonly know as halation. On top of this slow emulsion we have a quick emulsion which will get into our shadows and pick up detail."[35]

Nonhalation plates would be used in long exposures when the camera was "stopped down" and could result in excellent images of rooms, including, in all likelihood, the General Electric image of the cutting room in the Rice & Hutchins shoe factory. The line of windows on the right otherwise would have prevented capture of details on the right. Such plates had to be developed in different ways from ordinary negatives. The normal developers were too strong and would "bring up our top emulsion far enough before we fairly get started on our lower one, and by the time our lower emulsion is developed properly our upper one will be over developed."[36] To slow the process, the photographer diluted the developer with equal parts of water and more than doubled the immersion time. This technique permitted the water to soften both layers of emulsion and allowed the chemical action to be distributed equally between them.

Although nonhalation plates required special handling, they could easily be developed on a mass production basis as long as they were processed separately from other plates. They were easily available to any commercial photographer, being widely advertised in the professional journals. They were indispensable for indoor work.

Outdoor photographs presented other kinds of problems. As a fourth and final example of a difficulty commercial cameramen routinely solved, consider images of store windows, which reflect everything in front of them, including the camera. Some artistic photographers, including Robert Frank and Walker Evans, have exploited this fact to create interminglings of window displays and passers-by, but the commercial photographer sought to eliminate the glass and present the goods. During the day he would erect a curtain behind the camera, "cutting off reflections by standing step ladders . . . near the curb, laying fish poles across them," and draping cloth over them. At night no screens were necessary, and an electrically lighted window like that at Lord and Taylor's New York store required fifteen to thirty minutes' exposure. During this time, "A flash made from one side will often help a good deal in giving you the detail of the outside of the window."[37] But by day or night windows always presented strong contrasts requiring nonhalation plates.

These four examples do not exhaust the range of situations that confronted commercial photographers in the first decades of the century, but they are typical problems. The General Electric Archives contain thousands of photographs of machines and products, industrial interiors, and store windows. Not always the most interesting pictures in the collection, they were nevertheless the daily production of the staff for half a century. Carrying their heavy view finder and graflex cameras, tripods, glass negative cases, and sets of lenses, they repeated a small repertory of shots. The subjects differed little from one another in size or interest, but the techniques needed to represent them as a manager or customer saw them varied a good deal. The camera case necessarily contained putty, gasoline, flannel, and magnesium ribbons, and the photographers used a wide range of makeshift aids such as ladders, packing boxes, newspaper, and sand. A good commercial photographer invented techniques to master particular problems. Working on a tight schedule, he succeeded best when the photograph appeared to be nothing but the object in ordinary light. He succeeded, in short, when the results suggested he had done nothing more than point the camera and snap the shutter.

I have described only a few representative techniques used in capturing a latent image, leaving virtually untouched the whole area of darkroom techniques. Yet even an apparent failure could be revived through a series of manipulations. One final example will suffice to make this point. George Hance recalled that he used a special method to doctor harsh, contrasty negatives. He began by bleaching out the negative in ferricyanide and bromide, converting the black parts of his negative to a yellowish brown, continuing until the image almost disappeared altogether. After rinsing off these chemicals, he immersed the negative in hydroquinone developer, "and by frequently working at the back of the plate, we will see the film is blackening in the shadows first, as the emulsion is thinner there. When they have built up or blackened, and merely the thick highlights are brownish yellow, we know the Ferricyanide is exhausted, except in these highlights, and then a rinse and put the negative into any hypo or fixing bath."[38] In this way a skilled photographer could reduce the contrasts in any negative to create a more pleasing effect.

Manipulation could continue in the printing stage as well, if necessary. The techniques of dodging and retouching were well known, and a host of other subtle transformations were also practiced. But the normal procedure for industrial photographers was to minimize these darkroom techniques because of the pressures of time and cost-effectiveness. The work of the darkroom was routinized and geared to the mass production of images. Ideally all the manipulation would occur when the original exposure was made in the field. Because the variations of subject matter could not be controlled, the most experienced served as photographers only after long apprenticeships in the darkroom and enlarging rooms. The photographer was expected to deliver a product that could be handled easily, not to create difficult or time-consuming problems for the rest of the staff. He needed to attain a high degree of unobtrusive professionalism.

This systematic professional self-effacement created a style that sharply divides commercial photography from other photography before 1930. In contrast to the impressionistic emphasis of pictorialism, for example, it emphasized an aesthetics of realism, through sharp focus, avoidance of unusual camera angles, and a factual style of presentation. Unlike most artistic photographers, commercial artists did not strive for illusions of uniqueness but sought to establish solidity of a predictable character. They usually placed their cameras at eye level, for example, to trade on their audience's usual experience of vision.

As a result commercial work may seem more objective than artistic photography. Other institutionally produced images, such as news photographs, also may seem to be less biased representations of reality. Therefore the ways in which all photographs necessarily reduce and shape their subjects need to be detailed. Even leaving aside the professional representation of the subject and considering the image as it appears to a viewer, there are seven fundamental transformations enacted in taking any photograph. The following list is condensed from Roman Gubern's analysis in *Mensajes Iconicos en la Cultura de Masas*:

1. Photographs abolish the third dimension, modifying perspective.

2. They limit space to a rectangle, whose form itself has been borrowed from the standard canvas proportions of painting.

3. They abolish movement, creating a stasis that appears real but does not exist in experience. (The action photographs of athletes, leaping or running in a frozen blur that suggests movement, are no exception.)

4. The granular nature of photographic films and papers limits the resolution of the image if it is enlarged. The message is ultimately discontinuous and incomplete.

5. In the case of black and white photographs such as those of the General Electric Archives, color is abolished, and a range of tones from black to white is substituted for it. In this substitution, tonal relations of balance and intensity are transformed, and clashes of color are neutralized.

6. The physical scale of representation is altered so that at times the correct form and size cannot be determined.

7. All of the senses but one are suppressed, abolishing sound, touch, smell, and taste, leaving only sight.[39]

Collectively these seven transformations severely reduce any photograph's ability to act as a pane of glass, or window, on any subject. Photographs are not faithful analogues but translations. This translation is then further transformed by the intentions of the photographer and the development and printing of the image. The picture is other than the scene from which it was abstracted; in Wittgenstein's words, "A picture can depict any reality whose form it has," but "a picture cannot, however, depict its pictorial form: it displays it."[40] The proper study of photography therefore must begin with pictorial form or with the manner of display, not with the content.

Pictorial form is not analogous to linguistic form, however. In photography there is nothing akin to the phoneme, or the smallest unit of meaning. In photography one finds no double articulation, no fixed number of elements (as in the alphabet) capable of being combined into a potentially infinite number of signs.[41] Since the units from which words are assembled find no analogue in photography, there can be no equivalent of a dictionary of images since there is no arbitrarily established yet fixed principle for organizing one. Photographic research cannot be closely modeled on linguistics, or vice-versa. Rather there are two forms of communication, language and photography, and a more general theory of semiotics subsumes both.

Roman Jakobson developed an early version of such a theory, general enough to apply to both. Jakobson divided any act of communication into six parts. For (1) the sender to reach, (2) the receiver, they require (3) a reliable contact, (4) an understood context, (5) a mutually understood code (not necessarily linguistic), and (6) a message.[42] As first formulated, it appeared as shown in figure 1. It is not difficult to critize and then to rewrite this original model today, and Umberto Eco and Thomas Sebeok have done so. For example, the code of the sender and the receiver may not be the same. As Eco points out, "Sometimes the addressee's entire system of cultural units (as well as the concrete circumstances in which he lives) legitimate an interpretation that the sender would never have foreseen."[43] A photograph taken in 1880 reaches a viewer today who necessarily interprets it in ways then unimaginable. As this critique suggests, the message is not a solid unit but rather a text where many different codes intertwine. This is particularly true of photography, which can include within a frame kinesic signals, words, and other signs, all at the same time.

It is clear that this model requires modification before it can be applied to photographic communication. Nevertheless it has great utility at the start of an investigation because it identifies major areas that must be examined. The model does not provide a methodology in itself but suggests the units of analysis that must be developed.

The most important revision of the model concerns the de-

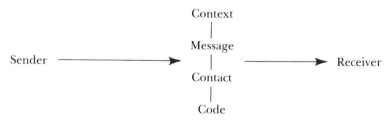

Figure 1.
General model of communication

ceptively simple notion of a sender. In conversation a single individual initiates an exchange, but in the case of much modern communication, including corporate photography, a group of individuals together construct and send a message. At General Electric the process was initiated by a request from outside the photographic department. The client decided on a particular subject to be depicted and then contacted the manager of the photographic unit, who assigned the job.[44] Usually the cameraman undertook the job as soon as possible, often the same day. The execution therefore is only the carrying out of an order, not a creative expression of personal taste. Another employee then developed the negative, and still another made the print before the work was sent back to the manager, who inspected it before forwarding it to the client. At least five persons were therefore involved in the initial creation of the print: the client, manager, photographer, developer, and printer. The message had hardly been sent, however, when all of these persons had been involved.

Any original photograph can be retouched, cropped, enlarged, made part of a montage, or subjected to many other operations once the client has it. The image taken in the initial exposure is akin to raw material that will be transformed into a product. It will be inserted into a particular context, given a label, and made part of a written story. This in turn will be part of a specific publication whose cover, publisher, and reputation add to the original message.

By the time a finished image has been sent, one cannot designate with certainty who is the creator; it is better to say that the corporation is the author. In specifying the sender, then, we have located a crucial aspect of industrial photographic communication: the sender is not a single intelligence but a set of bureaucratically ordered people. These senders perform specialized tasks for pay, with little control over the product. Image production is routinized and standardized. Possibly the entire process of sending a photographic message occurs without any discussion of that message or of the code being used.

Routinized production usually implies an assembly line, where workers churn out virtually identical goods. But photographs present a rather special case. Although they may eventually be replicated in the mass production process of magazine printing, these images must vary to be effective. Where the assembly line imposes standards of exact dimensions, management required less stringent requirements for photographers, who could use whatever techniques they wished as long as they achieved a specified result. For each of the in-house clients, the pictorial form had to be as constant as possible. Unlike the artistic photographer the industrial craftsman did not strive for unique effects but rather created a solid, workmanlike image of a predictable character.

The industrial aesthetic of the early twentieth century emphasizes realism, sharp focus, the avoidance of special effects, and a factual style of presentation. Industrial photographs trade on the notion that seeing is believing, that things are as they appear. Generally no solarization, double exposure, or special printing techniques were used. The successful industrial image makes the subject easily apparent and allows the viewer to forget that it has been interpreted in any way. Perhaps for this reason mirrors are seldom used to show more than one side of a scene since they introduce variance and potential multiplicity into what is intended to be a single, clear view of the subject.

Paradoxically a multiplicity of hands turns out a limited range of photographs. In contrast the artist photographer, working alone, seeks to create new images and startle the audience, even at the risk of losing it. Without managerial control and without the need to work with others (particularly the printer and developer), the artistic photographer is free to experiment, wait, take a great deal of time, and try special equipment. As a result the great artistic photographers reinterpret familiar objects, allowing us to see them in new ways. Edward Weston's pictures of artichokes, peppers, toilets, and other ordinary objects transformed them into sculptural forms.[45] His work, like that of other artists, exemplifies the re-creation of an object that has become familiar. By presenting the object in a strikingly new manner, this defamiliarization forces viewers to encounter the object as if for the first time. Industrial photography strives for precisely the opposite effect; it presents new objects in such a manner that they appear familiar.

In short, industrial photography strives for a mundane realism, and its success often looks like aesthetic failure. Time pressure and the division of image production into specialized tasks do not by themselves account for the appearance of the images. Rather management maintains a standardized rhetorical consistency through constant monitoring. Its surveillance does not mean, however, that managers consciously understand photography as a coded system of communication. Discussions with current General Electric personnel suggest that they view both the archives and their current production as a vast series of idiosyncratic images rather than as photographs that fall into a delimited number of categories.[46] This perception results from their interest in the varied subjects that are assigned rather than in the standardized aspects of the work. Their routinized techniques give consistency to the images they produce. Both managers and photographers therefore seem to be using a code without being aware that it exists, comparable to the famous Molière character who does not know that he is speaking prose. To perform their jobs satisfactorily, they do not need consciously to know the categories of photographic communication they employ.

The industrial photographic system can be understood as a structure without the double articulation of a language but with a unique form of double coding. These two codes are each controlled by different groups in the factory hierarchy. Management imposes the subject matter; the photographers impose the technical code appropriate to frame the subject matter.[47] In this system it is not necessary for either side to comprehend the other's coding procedures. Management knows what it wants in the sense that some pictures will be acceptable and others not, but it chooses without understanding the means used to attain satisfactory images. Similarly, the photographers do not need to know what meaning will be assigned to an image or to whom it will be addressed. They engage in routinized activities; based on experience, they know roughly what sort of image is wanted when they receive an assignment.

The image is not sent in a single action but rather processed. The sender consists of two groups, each employing a different code to make a single message. Together they shape virtually every aspect of the communication situation: the photographic contact, the context within which the message will appear, the contents of the message, and the two codes, technical and secondary. Such photography is hidden from its audience and at best only partially visible to the senders. Jakobson's diagram must therefore be drastically redrawn to express this situation (figure 2).

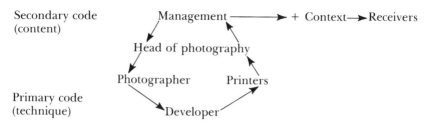

Figure 2.
Industrial photographic communication

Industrial photography presents an unusual communication situation due to its double coding. Because management controls the photography department, this double coding does not result in confusion or inappropriate synthesis of techniques and contents. Management both initiates and concludes the process of sending the message. Managerial control includes far more than mere direction over the process of producing the image. Once the photograph was ready, management inserted it in carefully chosen media. These newspapers and magazines addressed particular markets, or groups of receivers, some inside the corporation and others outside it. In short, the corporation decided who should receive each message. Not every photograph would be shown to every possible viewer. Instead the company's editors selectively reached each of the major groups it found important. Thus they had to define discrete audiences—engineers, workers, managers, consumers—and the subject matter appropriate to each.

Because the appropriate subjects varied, editors required quite different kinds of photographs for each publication. Their requests came to the photographers, however, in terms of subject matter. The photographers selected a technique for each subject and sought whenever possible to adhere to formulas already worked out. They did not invent a new procedure each time they were asked to photograph an executive or an inventor. Technically their productions fell within a limited number of image classes. These groups of photographs treated a given subject—machinery, workers, visitors, products—in stylized ways. Workers were never shot in the same manner as inventors, for example, and products for mass consumption were treated quite differently from industrial goods. Such consistencies can be discovered only through comparison and contrast between image classes. Otherwise only the specificity and the secondary coding of a single image are visible; subject matter imposed by management overwhelms the photographers' techniques. The comparative method thus exposes the central problem most critics create for themselves when they look within but a single frame. They accept the content as depicted. As a result, for example, Roland Barthes arrived at the mistaken conclusion that photography is a message without a code. In an often reprinted essay he proclaimed:

In order to move from the reality to its photograph it is in no way necessary to divide up this reality into units and to constitute these units as signs, substantially different from the object they communicate; there is no necessity to set up a relay, that is to say a code, between the object and its image. Certainly the image is not the reality but at least it is its perfect analogon and it is exactly this analogical perfection which, to common sense, defines the photography. This can be seen in the special status of the photographic image: it is a message without a code; from which proposition an important corollary must immediately be drawn: the photographic message is a continuous message.[48]

Because Barthes looked carefully only within the frames of single images, he was led to a series of interconnected errors. He is correct, of course, to say that there is no need to set up a relay between an object and its photograph. But this does not mean that no coding exists; rather it means that the viewer and the photographer share a common secondary code. Both have lived in the world and know the names and uses of objects; both know languages and so forth. They hardly approach the photograph without a code. More crucially, however, the framing of the image is also a coded phenomenon, imposing a set of constraints on the image's meaning. These constraints are not only those of the standardized rectangular frame borrowed from painting at photography's inception (whereas a circular frame might have been used, for example) but also those of focus, distance from the object, and the like, not to mention what is thereby excluded. He is thus quite wrong to conclude that the photographic message is a continuous message because such a generalization applies only to the space enclosed by a single frame. Reflection will show that any photograph is a fragment, continuous with nothing. Finally, Barthes is wrong to say that a photograph is a perfect analogon of its object, even within the frame, for the seven reasons cited by Roman Gubern.

What then is one to make of the many incisive analyses Barthes has made of particular images? They are studies of the secondary coding, a gloss on the objects represented, not on the means of representation. These critiques—one thinks particularly of his early essay in *Mythologies* dealing with a black soldier on the cover of *Match*—offer a valuable lesson in the reading of individual photographs.[49] But what also must be accomplished is the more fundamental determination of the forms of primary, or technical coding, for these define the space within which idiosyncratic contents are deployed.

In concrete terms the manner in which an executive is posed, lighted, and photographed is a constant in the General Electric Archives, but this becomes clear only through comparative analysis. Viewing but a single image forces one to examine the secondary coding: the specific executive, his clothing, hair, height, and photogenia. When a large number of images can be identified as being similar in technique, however varied their contents (black executives, women executives, old and young executives, and so forth), they constitute a class with regularities that can be specified. Once several classes have been identified, one can supplement the sort of analysis Barthes developed. For as soon as a number of classes are examined together, their differences define a field of oppositions, which have been consistently imposed. This field defines General Electric's ideology with regard to the photographic subjects and registers shifts in that ideology as the company addresses different audiences.

The image classes at General Electric are not an isolated phenomenon. Although no master code underlies all photography, it must be understood as a field of discourse where many opposed statements can be made. Corporate photography stands as a central practice in the image making of the twentieth century, not on qualitative grounds but because of its wide distribution and because of its capacity to assimilate other styles, particularly those of documentary cameramen but also those employed by freelance artistic photographers. From this perspective photography as a whole emerges not as a codeless form of direct communication, as Barthes would have it, but as a web of contradictory encodations.

The modified Jakobson model permits comparison among

these different modes of photographic communication. For example, artistic photography contrasts with corporate work at almost every point. The independent artist controls not only the shooting but the development and printing of the image; the commercial worker is on a team that collectively exercises minimal control over the subject matter. The artist inserts completed prints in quite different contexts—museums and galleries rather than business magazines.[50] Perhaps the most telling difference among these kinds of photography lies in their use of codes. The commercial emphasis on apparent realism and transparency in the message militates against any visible tampering with the subject's appearance in the final print. The photographers will make enormous efforts to attain a desired appearance, but this labor must be entirely effaced in the content of the image. In contrast the artistic photographer not only allows the camera work to intrude into the end result but makes these techniques a legible part of his vocabulary, part of a personal stamp set on the subject. Double exposures, solarization, special printing techniques, hand-made paper, toning baths, and a host of other materials and techniques are not only permitted but encouraged, with one important caveat: the artistic photographer generally is not encouraged to manipulate the scene photographed but only to stretch and explore the technical means of depiction itself. This prohibition was especially strong in the first half of the twentieth century. Commercial and artistic photography thus inverted one another's practices. The artist emphasized a legible but pure technique while refusing to tamper with the subject; the commercial craftsman treated the subject matter cavalierly, rearranging it to suit a preconceived idea of the object while effacing all visible traces of artistry. The artist emphasized the code; the commercial photographer, the message.

Working with Jakobson's (modified) model, the distinctive features of many forms of photography can be specified. The early commercial photographer emphasized the image's context, giving a product meaning through associations, and stressed the audience while effacing himself. The image must appear to be the structural limit. If a viewer asks who took the photograph, then it is being treated as art; interest has shifted from the product to the artist. Such a shift is desirable only in a special case, such as high fashion, where the photographer's name can add luster to the product itself, as in Richard Avedon's work.[51] Except for such cases, where the photographer becomes an attribute of the product, commercial images are matters of context and audience.

Corporate image making can be further defined through a second comparison, this time with a form with a similar origin and subject material. The emergence of documentary photography, exemplified in the work of Jacob Riis and Lewis Hine, can be directly traced to the dry plate negative and halftone process that made commercial photography possible. The documentary photographer also worked for an institution or organization, and work in this genre was also disseminated through magazine publication, in many cases by the *Survey Graphic*. The difference between corporate and documentary work lay in their varying approaches to closely related subject matter rather than being the result of differing technical processes.

Both Lewis Hine and anonymous General Electric photographers made images of the southern textile mills between 1900 and 1910. Hine's photographs emphasize the people in these mills, particularly the children, who worked amid dust and potentially injurious machinery. He often used a long perspective view, in which the rows of looms with their repetitive spindles create a line that recedes toward a distant wall. A child stands at the midpoint of this line, all of which he or she must continually tend and keep in running order. In "The Boss Teaches a Young Spinner in a North Carolina Mill," Hine depicts the scene from a child's eye level, showing the dominance of the boss, the safety hazards, and the repetitiveness of the task.[52] General Electric photographers depicted virtually identical mills in quite different ways. They eliminated the workers and emphasized the machinery, usually electric motors that the company had installed. Instead of Hine's receding line of looms, which blur into the distance behind the child, General Electric's looms cross the center of the frame, each in sharp focus.[53] Instead of Hine's dirty floor and the fiber-filled air, a clean room and a pleasant ambiance. Hine's work calls out for social reform: cleaner factories, safer machines, and an end to child labor. The corporation's work celebrates electrification and industrial progress, making no visual reference to the workers.

As this contrast indicates, corporate photography contains a latent ideology. Corporate images did not result automatically from changes in photographic technology. Rather companies used the new forms of photography to make apparently factual statements about the world. Their images emphasized property rather than persons, progress rather than social problems, managerial rather than working-class perspectives. As these contrasts emphasize, no matter how complete one's understanding of photography as a changing technology, it must also be seen as the production and distribution of ideology. The General Electric cameramen mastered their medium; they could create many different messages beginning with any given subject material. But the ideology expressed in these photographs remained latent so far as the cameramen themselves were concerned. Performing routinized labor, neither they nor their professional journals conceived of image making as being more than a set of techniques to be put at the service of clients.

The following chapters examine the audiences that management chose to address, placing the photographs made for each group in their social and economic contexts. Beginning at the turn of the century, management discovered the need to address four quite distinct groups: engineers, blue-collar workers, managers, and consumers. In each case economic exigencies, labor conflicts, and other problems combined to suggest the creation of new kinds of photographs to address an audience. No overall strategy appears to have been mapped out in advance; rather managers acted in response to changing conditions. Nevertheless, by 1930 General Electric and other major corporations had created a massive system of image production and distribution. That system played an important role in the construction of varying image worlds.

General Electric Photographic Studio, c. 1895, interior

General Electric Photographic Studio, c. 1895, exterior

William Sellers & Company, Boring Mill, c. 1895

Domestic Range, c. 1920

Cutting Room, Rice & Hutchins, South Braintree, c. 1915

Lord & Taylor's Window, New York, c. 1920

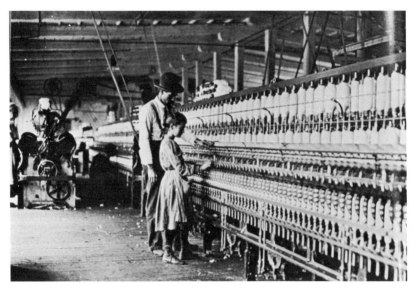

The Boss Teaches a Young Spinner in a North Carolina Mill. Photo by
Lewis Hine, 1908. Reprinted courtesy of the George Eastman House.

Cotton Mill, interior, before 1900

II

The Receivers

4

Engineers: The Corporation as Science

Business publications in the United States long antedated the formation of General Electric in 1892. In the second half of the eighteenth century newspapers of one or two pages specifically designed for merchants first appeared. Called price currents, they reported "changes in commodity prices, movements of ships, and fluctuations in the rates of exchange." Fifteen of these were founded before 1800, each issued from a port city, the majority coming from Philadelphia. They were edited by "commodity brokers, commission merchants, or printers" and read by wholesalers and merchants. They connected a loose aggregation of individuals primarily for the exchange and not the manufacture of goods.[1]

Before the 1830s the U.S. economy was largely agricultural, and no individual business or trade required a specialized publication. But with industrialization new kinds of information were necessary. Three new types of periodical appeared between 1830 and the Civil War. First, mechanization called for trade papers in particular industries. Among the first such publications were those for railroads, the *American Railroad Journal* (1832–present), and iron goods, the *Hardwareman's Newspaper and American Manufacturer's Circular* (1855–present; now called *Iron Age*).[2] Such magazines provided technical information to a specialized audience in contrast to the shorter and more general price currents. They reached an audience spread across the nation rather than in a single locality.

Of equal importance to business were technical and scientific journals that fostered the spread of knowledge. One of the earliest was the *Journal of the Philadelphia College of Pharmacy*, founded in 1825, and followed almost immediately by the *Journal of the Franklin Institute* (1826). Others soon appeared, notably *Scientific American* (1845). A measure of their utility was that most survived to the present day.[3]

More sporadically successful were labor magazines, first published in New York in the 1820s and soon after in Philadelphia and Boston. These served the new class of skilled artisans and craftsmen known as mechanics, who worked in the emerging industries. These were not blue-collar workers in today's sense of the term. They controlled the pace of their work, for example, and claimed many privileges in the shop, where they did not punch a time clock. This same independence, combined with their employment by many small companies, however, undermined cooperation. Their magazines seldom survived more than a few years.[4]

As small-scale capitalism gave way to corporate monopolies during the nineteenth century, magazines controlled by a single company became possible. The *General Electric Review* was a characteristic product of this stage and would not have served any useful purpose much earlier. While the older technical journals and trade papers continued and the large companies supported them in many ways, other forums were useful to address employees and professional groups. Many companies therefore started in-house magazines to fill the growing void between management and labor. The form of these magazines varied a great deal, depending on whom the companies wished to address.

By the 1950s General Electric issued seven quite different publications to reach audiences that together totaled more than a quarter of a million persons a month. It had become the largest single corporate publisher in the United States. Starting with the *Review* in 1903, it later developed *Works News* (blue-collar workers, 1917), *Monogram* (managers, 1922), *General Electric News Graphic* (appliance salesmen, 1922), *Light* (lighting specialists, 1923), and *G.E. Digest* (overseas personnel, 1924).[5] Each addressed a single audience, as had the trade publications and scientific journals. But the communication situation was not identical. In the period of small-scale capitalism, information flowed between equals. These new corporate magazines came from powerful managers to their dependents inside the corporation or to professional groups particularly involved with the company. Executives controlled every aspect of the communication, designating format, content, and audience.

Just as photographers created images in accord with previously established conceptions of their subjects, writers and editors shaped entire magazines to serve General Electric's goals. Earlier business publications had been specialized only according to industry or to a specific branch of knowledge. The new corporate magazines were specialized in accord with the needs of single corporations.

General Electric Review served as a prototype for specialized publication inside the company. Like it, each of the others would be developed as a form appropriate to a particular market. In the *Review*, whose audience primarily was to be engineers, the editors imitated the form of an objective scientific journal. They could thus influence crucially important professionals, while conforming to their standards. The *Review*'s targets were the new corps of engineers, whose numbers in the United States grew from but 8,000 in 1880 to 136,000 in 1920. The area of electrical engineering in particular expanded from virtually nothing in 1880 to a sizable sector in a single generation. The first electrical engineers were often as not outside the academy, the most knowledgeable being those who worked with Edison, Thompson, and other inventors. The demand for engineers was too sudden, however, for the corporations themselves to educate 125,000 in a single generation, and they encouraged universities to train as many engineers as possible.[6]

Yet corporations did not wish entirely to lose control of the educational process. Through a variety of means they sought to shape the new profession. These included funding university research, political influence, creation of private research laboratories, and establishment of postgraduate courses. Using all of these means General Electric helped to define the role of the engineers. And in this effort, *General Electric Review* was a key element.

As David Noble has pointed out in *America by Design*, in the early twentieth century American engineering might have developed in at least three different directions. The first of these "might have stressed the business-leadership function of engineering, giving rise to a type of businessmen's association." Another option might have been "engineers as corporate employees," in which case they would have formed trade unions. But a third definition proved dominant, although elements of these first two possibilities remained. It "emphasized the scientific nature of engineering and inspired a professional identity grounded upon the monopoly of esoteric knowledge, similar to that of lawyers, physicians, and scientists."[7]

General Electric chose to stress this third conception insistently in *General Electric Review*, which began publication in 1903. It soon reached a circulation of 6,000, which remained steady until after World War II. During this half-century it helped to define the profession by reaching important educators at major engineering schools such as the Massachusetts Institute of Technology, Stanford, and Michigan State. Yet the *Review* eschewed many topics engineers were interested in, particularly social reform and scientific management. Edwin Layton's *The Revolt of the Engineers: Social Responsibility and the American Engineering Profession* explored how during these same years engineers adopted many of the causes of progressive reform as a logical extension of their work.[8] Had the *Review* accurately reflected the general discussion and debate within the profession between 1903 and 1950, it would have contained many articles on scientific management and the application of engineering to social problems. The magazine might have carried notes on the national meetings of organizations such as the American Society of Mechanical Engineers or the American Society of Engineering Educators. By avoiding all reference to these organizations or to any of the debates within the profession, the *Review* opted for the narrowest and most instrumental view of the engineer, or the one that, in Noble's words, "inspired a professional identity grounded upon the monopoly of esoteric knowledge."

The magazine served purposes besides those of circumscribing the profession. Many of its readers were outside the academy, occupying influential positions as engineers with municipal power plants, state advisory boards, and private industry. All of these persons were potential customers for General Electric products. In the period before World War I the electrical business had not yet diversified. Most orders were for heavy equipment, not consumer goods, as the electrical companies focused on expanding their service to the smaller cities and towns. Electrical stoves, refrigerators, and washing machines had not yet come on the market. Thus the company's salesmen dealt largely with customers for heavy equipment, most of whom either were electrical engineers or businessmen influenced by them. The Great White Ways that cities bought to illuminate downtown areas between 1911 and 1930 exemplify expensive systems sold as units. While politicians and local businessmen had to be convinced on the basis of appearances, engineers demanded detailed knowledge of the electrical system, and in most cases they ultimately decided which kinds of equipment to buy.

General Electric also had a vital interest in the electrification of heavy industry, where an enormous conversion occurred in the first three decades of the twentieth century. In 1899 only 5 percent of all manufacturing horsepower was electrical. By 1929 electricity supplied 80 percent of all horsepower, and production capacity had mushroomed. Electric motors were far more versatile than any other form of power generation. They were an essential part of assembly line manufacturing, for example, permitting plant managers to arrange machines in any order, without concern for how the power from a pulley, belt, or steam pipe might reach them. For the first time the sequence of work could be rearranged on short notice as the power from small electrical motors drove each machine. But although electricity was a superior form of power for manufacturing, this fact did not guarantee that General Electric's motors would be preferred to those of competitors.[9]

Thus the company published the *Review* for several audiences. Not only did it influence undergraduates studying engineering, it reached the technicians and officials who would buy and maintain turbines, generators, transformers, power lines, and the many electrical devices that linked these machines into systems. Although the company did reach both groups through advertisements in the trade publications, such as *Electric Age, Electrical World,* and *Electric Street Railway,* the *Review* provided information too complex for inclusion in advertising, and, more important, it packaged that information in an apparently scientific format.[10]

However, the magazine had not originally been planned to serve these ends. Rather it started as a confidential in-house publication addressed to salesmen. At first the home office issued a series of newsletters and circulars to them, as they were needed, from 1892 until 1903. These explained the product line and gave instructions on installation and maintenance. As the business grew, these haphazard publications became unsatisfactory, and the Publicity Bureau was instructed to begin a regular magazine. At first only insiders were permitted to see it. Early issues contained this warning on the title page: "Confidential: For the Information of Officers and Employees of this Company only."[11] In the beginning *General Electric Review* openly discussed new contracts, current research, and other sensitive information it did not want broadcast generally. Yet its fundamental concerns were the same then as they would be later: favorable publicity and sales. The editor advised readers, "Reference to important installations or large contracts secured will influence prospective customers."[12] Salesmen also were expected to share the magazine's technical information with buyers. In short, secrecy was incompatible with sales.

When the company removed the stricture of confidentiality in the following year, however, the magazine's content began to change. If salesmen were free to give away copies to customers, articles had to deemphasize the internal concerns of the corporation and offer material interesting to the engineering profession as a whole. The editors had selected the strategy of imitating a scientific journal, drawing on the growing body of specialists at the company's new research and development laboratory, which included some men of international reputation, among them, Charles Proteus Steinmetz. The typical issue included at least one article from a scientist, along with stories of new installations and sales.[13]

By 1908 the magazine's transformation was complete, and it became available to the public for a subscription of three dollars a year. Appearing monthly it no longer seemed a corporate publication but a specialized periodical of interest to electrical engineers. Even the name served this purpose, since both *general* and *electric* might appear to an unwary reader as adjectives rather than proper nouns. As a general review concerned with electricity, it claimed a general audience. An editorial asserted that each issue "should be of interest to the construction engineer, to the operator, to the central station man, the consulting engineer, and the student."[14] Note that two of the most important groups of readers, salesmen and their customers, were conspicuously omitted from the list. Neither would ever be directly addressed in the magazine, except in avowed advertisements, which themselves were few in number. These advertisements assisted the illusion that the magazine was a technical review.

In fact customers were the principal targets of many articles. A sample issue dealt with such topics as commercial electric testing, transmission line calculations, and Rosenberg generators. The *Review* also ran articles serially, such as one entitled "Transmission Line Constants," which ran over seven issues. As these topics indicate, the principal concern of the articles was power generation and transmission. Indeed once electrical systems had been installed across the United States (by about 1945), General Electric had no more need for the magazine and stopped publishing it.

The *Review*'s origin and demise demonstrate that the magazine's purpose was to generate corporate profits and that it offered information as a means to an end rather than as an end in itself. Nevertheless, the magazine's format made it appear to be a scientific journal. It used high-quality paper that suggested permanent value. It printed articles two columns to the page, and its layout was plain and unobtrusive, with no eye-catching designs. Each article was a self-contained unit, with no continuing pages in other sections. Advertising never intruded into the articles, and the few advertisements often came from other companies. Although in many cases these outsiders were suppliers to General Electric, their presence seemed to establish the *Review* as a open forum. Overall the magazine's layout signaled that it was a disinterested, educational periodical rather than an in-house organ, with a goal of profits.

Indeed one editorial explicitly compared the *Review* with an academic journal and found three similarities between the company and the university: both gave courses to graduates of technical schools, both sponsored research work, and both published their results: "As the large university prints its theses, monographs, and pamphlets, so the manufacturing concern publishes the results of recent developments and improvements in engineering methods and practices." The editorial thus concluded that the *Review*'s function was clear: "it is the medium for disseminating this information to the engineering profession."

Such a statement places the corporation outside the marketplace. It hides the origin of the magazine as a salesmen's newsletter and appropriates the prestige of the university and of science to create the impression that General Electric had little interest in money. Appropriately the magazine's articles did not deal with profits, losses, dividends, sales meetings, labor problems, or other economic matters. The content, like the format, imitated the best scholarly journals. The *Review* presented new company products as part of human progress; its editors described hydroelectric dams in India or Oregon not as major contracts but as the march of an inevitable historical process. In retrospect electrification may seem inevitable but not the sale of General Electric machines to supply the majority of the energy. Nor was it necessary that an advanced economy use as much power as the United States has in the twentieth century. In part as a result of the success of *General Electric Review*, U.S. energy use per capita increased 250 percent between 1900 and 1955.[15]

The *Review* was the first monthly publication the photographic department had to provide with illustrations. Despite the apparent breadth of the possible subjects, however, the photographers managed to insert most of them in only five image classes. Together these five made up 85 percent of all the *Review*'s images.[16] In different ways, each class enhanced the scientific and objective demeanor of the magazine as much as the content of the articles or the layout. Indeed in the photographs format and content became inseparable.

The editors most frequently used images that depicted company products out of context.[17] This class invariably showed a machine against a white background. The photographer manipulated the light to eliminate shadows and contours from the surrounding space and used a hard, sharp focus. In the most literal sense one could never see anything like the image that resulted. Such photographs originated in mechanical drawings, which in the past had provided similar abstract depictions of machines. The photographs that imitate these drawings are extremely cold and possess the appearance of geometrical shapes. They make visible the scientific spirit that suffused the magazine. Here was the object as pure information, with no surrounding context, as in "Arc Welder Generator Direct Connected to Induction Motor" and "300 Amp. 12000 Volt Electrically Operated Oil Switch." Their shadowless white backgrounds suggest objects without connection to history, to individuals, to time, or to social values.

Given this presentation of the object, the editor's captions did not dispel the illusion of an industrial thing in itself. The captions were invariably static and seldom contained a verb or a completed thought. The editors named the object but did not give it a context or suggest how it had been created. Nor did the authors deal with these matters in the accompanying articles, which concerned only how the machine worked.

In the second most common class of images—machines installed in power plants, factories, and other industrial sites— the editors used similar labeling conventions.[18] The photographs never contained people and always put a product in the center of the frame. Although these generators, turbines, and other electrical equipment normally were surrounded by workers, in the images the machines stood alone. Such photographs accompanied articles about installation, but neither they nor their accompanying stories suggested any connection between engineering and society.

While both of these image classes persisted from the first years of the *General Electric Review* until its demise, neither was common in other company magazines. Workers never saw abstract images of machines, and engineers almost never saw workers, who appear only in shots of large machines, to provide a sense of scale. These images were rarely needed, but when used, they occupied a prominent place in the magazine, such as the cover or frontispiece. The men function as units of measurement, not as individuals, and so are never identified by name. Usually between two and five workers appear, but they never pose as central subjects. They do not hold the tools used to create the machine, nor do they seek to dominate it in their postures. Often they stand with backs to the camera, with the machine the center of attention. The men may link hands and curve their bodies around its sides, stand on one anothers' shoulders, or merely stand with face averted, as in "Transformers in Testing Pit" and "Bucket Wheel for G.E. Steam Turbine."[19] These postures, which executives and inventors never take, express subordination. The *Review*'s use of these images at points of maximum visibility underlines a message never articulated there in words. It reveals something latent in the magazine's emphasis on products in isolation: that constructing the machine has no dignity and that those who perform manual work are appendages to the industrial process. There are no images of engineers with dirty hands. The magazine encouraged them to think of themselves as a separate class and to dwell on scientific progress. Its articles contemplated either theory or finished systems but not the work required to transform theory into practice.

This theoretical emphasis may be found again in the profusion of charts and graphs that fill the *Review*. These, together with the abstract product photographs, establish a dominant tone. They suggest a world of hard facts and irrefutable proofs, which have no relation to sales, profits, the work force, or consumers. The only inhabitants of this world, other than occasional workers needed to provide a sense of scale, are the engineers themselves. Significantly they almost never appear in context, working with machinery. Rather they appear in small portraits, usually as the authors of articles. Invariably they wear coat and tie, clear signs of their status above the workers as members of a professional class. Indeed that professionalism could be seen in the images of scientists who staffed the new Research and Development Laboratories, headed by Willis R. Whitney, whose portrait was made in the same way.[20]

The only other kind of images that occur with any frequency in the *Review* are group portraits of several engineers. As in the individual portraits, however, the men (there are no women) stand against a neutral background rather than at a production site.[21]

These five classes of images—abstract machines, installations of products, machines with workers used for scaling, and the two kinds of portraits—gave readers an extremely reduced idea of General Electric as a whole. Through them engineers could hardly have been reminded that the company employed tens of thousands of workers, that scientific management was a prominent new theory, or that some engineers believed their profession ought to take on political responsibilities. Rather the photographs overwhelmingly emphasized machines cut off from human involvement and from their social implications. Fully 70 percent of all the *Review* images fell into the first two image classes.[22]

Such an unvarnished view of individual objects also can be found in the photography of Edward Weston, who at times explored an individual subject against a white background.[23] But in his work light plays a much different role, eliminating some features by casting them into shadow, highlighting others, and giving his subjects an immanence lacking in the work of the photographic department. The camera for him was a means to transcend the ordinary appearance of objects. His images of cauliflowers, peppers, and other vegetables transform these everyday objects. Nor were these transformations limited to subjects from the natural world such as fruits and vegetables. He worked equally well with ordinary hardware. Toilet bowls became sculptural forms; machines metamorphosed into formal patterns.

In contrast, although the General Electric photographers also worked with a single object against a white background, their images achieve an opposite effect. They do not invite the imagination. They present a series of industrial essences, reified and separated from an immanent relationship with the world. Such solitary objects, cut off from any trace of history or society, are irreducible units to which meanings can be added but from which nothing can be taken away. One cannot imagine anything less metaphorical than these hard-edged outlines, which are never compromised by a technique that might draw attention to itself.

This comparison reveals the extent to which the objectivity of the *General Electric Review* was an adopted style, a choice that implied the ideology of professionalism and scientific expertise rather than social involvement. The magazine expressed a false objectivity about the industrial process, presenting it as a mere by-product of technological innovation. It encouraged engineers to think about their work as the automatic result of research and development, as something to which the rest of society responded without question, without resistance. In this vision the worker dwindled to near insignificance. The *Review* thereby reinforced class distinctions between engineers and workers not only through its instrumental choice of audience but also through images that told that audience how to see itself. They were told to envision themselves as part of management, as thinkers in coats and ties, as members of a new industrial elite.

The studied objective stance of the magazine had many uses. It served as a covert form of advertising, allowing the company to market its scientific expertise as educational material. It helped to shape the engineer's professional identity. It reinforced class distinctions. Photography served all three of these goals. While individual images might be considered accurate, the limited range of photographs and their stylistic repetition provided neither balance nor objectivity but an extremely narrow view of the company's interests and of the engineering profession. While cultivating the appearance of scientific objectivity, the magazine in fact served to restrict comprehension of the social dimensions of the electrical revolution.

The form of later company publications would change in accord with audience and marketing objectives, but as in the *General Electric Review*, photographs played a central role in shaping the magazine. The image classes deployed in one seldom appeared in another, yet individual images retained their apparent validity as realistic descriptions of the world. It followed that anything written might be documented in photographs; any signifier could be paired with an invented signified. General Electric had attained a kind of power unequaled in previous business publications and impossible before the development of large corporations. It could select the audience, message, contact, context, and code, effectively controlling virtually all of the communication. And through photography it could provide an appearance of realism and objectivity that made each message seem to be the truth.

The truth of vision in such corporate photography did not resemble current practice in artistic circles. At the time when the *Review* began publication, Alfred Stieglitz and many others were committed to pictorialism, an impressionist-inspired form of photography, in which soft focus lenses and special papers or printing processes were used to create images with no hard edges or details.[24] Pictorialism remained dominant until World War I, by which time Stieglitz had begun to turn away from it to champion straight photography, to be advocated later by Weston and the f 64 group. The origin of the corporate style thus would appear to have been the tradition of mechanical drawing and illustration, not artistic photography. Only in the 1920s would a group of precisionist painters and photographers such as Charles Sheeler and Charles Demuth make a machine aesthetic well known.[25] But their work, strongly influenced by cubism, had no discernible influence on the *Review*, whose routinized images continued in subsequent decades, whenever possible, to follow the pattern established before 1910. Changes in photographic techniques did occur, but the appearance of the images did not. Yet if the *Review*'s appearance remained static, new publications for other groups soon required new strategies of representation.

Arc Welder Generator Direct Connected to Induction Motor

300 Amp. 12000 Volt Electrically Operated Oil Switch

Power Station, c. 1900

Indiana and Michigan Electric Company Transformer, High Voltage
Side, 1923

Transformers in Testing Pit, 1923

Bucket Wheel for G.E. Steam Turbine, Assembled for Factory Inspection, 1931

Portrait of Dr. Willis R. Whitney, c. 1910

5

Workers: The Corporation as Community

The General Electric *Works News* is best understood against the publishing background outlined in chapter 4. The same changes in industrial organization made both it and the *General Electric Review* useful tools. When price currents gave way to trade papers and technical journals, another sporadic form of publishing had also appeared, worker magazines. Although unsuccessful in the pre–Civil War era, they became more common and longer lived as the numbers of industrial workers increased. And just as General Electric imitated the objectivity of the scientific journal in addressing engineers, it adopted the facade of a labor magazine in addressing workers. It took the company much longer to begin such a magazine, however. The *Review* had developed directly from newsletters to salesmen and served an immediately evident purpose. But the company published nothing for its blue-collar work force for a quarter-century (1892–1917). When it did begin a magazine, it responded not to a sales opportunity but to an apparent threat to control over the labor force.

A pronounced division between labor and management took a generation to develop. When Edison and the other pioneers in the electrical industry began the companies that eventually became General Electric, they knew their employees personally. The shops were small, and work functions had not yet been divided up. It would have been ludicrous for early managers to publish a magazine for workers whom they saw every day face to face. They could communicate easily with them at any time. Photographs were taken on occasion; they depicted the familiar work rooms and those who labored there daily. They were formal reminders of personal associations and sprang from the same impulse that leads any small group to make a picture of itself. The image's subjects are at once the senders and receivers.[1]

As business increased, the social distance between workers and management also increased. Managers no longer posed with their employees but instead ordered formal portraits. By 1895 when the Schenectady works had 6,000 workers, the photographs showed groups whose work was far more defined and specialized than that at Menlo Park in 1880. By the later date only individual shops and departments appeared together, as in "Punch and Die Department," an example of those transitional worker images when the unity of management and labor had begun to erode. This erosion can be discerned only in contrast with later images. If these men are not in their shop, the image reveals considerable independence for the workers themselves. Male employees do not wear uniforms but express personal taste in their dress. They choose their poses, crossing their arms, donning hats, gazing into or away from the camera, at their pleasure. As was the case at Menlo Park, where Edison posed with his assistants, the foreman does not stand out from the others.[2]

The photographs of women taken in the same years show their far more dependent role in the workplace. They have a male foreman and work at far less independent jobs than the men. While it might be tempting to read their folded hands and less individualistic poses as signs of feminine submission to male authority, their images should not be read so simply. They performed repetitive, unskilled work. They could be replaced far more easily than the men, and their average period of service at the company was much shorter than that of any other group of workers. Thus for a variety of reasons they had less independence than the men, and indeed, within a generation, as the corporation gained more control over the workplace, the differences between male and female poses would diminish.[3] Where in the 1890s male workers made independent statements in posing, by the 1920s that freedom would largely be gone. The archives contain virtually no individualistic images after 1910. Gone with them were the strong poses that indicated the worker's sense of self-importance. The early photographs had paid the respect craftsmen demanded, in such photographs as "Workers in Transformer Shop" from 1893. Here they appear in the workplace as those who control it. They are not forced to stand in artificial symmetry or pose as convenient measures of scale. Rather, this is their space, with their coats hung along the left side and their tools in their hands. Such group portraits of master craftsmen virtually disappeared in later years.

At the same time workers also had virtually disappeared from another class of image common in the first decade. Early photographs of factory life had often imitated the conventions of magazine illustration. Such engravings generally included human figures to provide interest in the industrial landscape and also to give the environment a human scale. In 1888, for example, *Electrical World* carried several of the Schenectady works, including "View of the Main Floor of the Wire Insulating Department."[4] But a few years later such images would have been reproduced using the halftone process, and the linkage between this older style of representation and corporate photography would necessarily remain conjectural. General Electric photographers made copies of these engravings and kept them on file as models to follow in making their own images. They copied the engraver's use of perspective and elevation above the factory floor in images made for managers but in the early years stayed at eye level just as often, showing the shops from a worker's perspective, as in "Wire and Cable Department, Schenectady Works, c. 1895." Comparison of these two images emphasizes the differences between engraving and photography. For the engraver light posed no problems, while for the photographer the bright windows and the dark floor created an almost insuperable contrast. The engraver also could edit out details to create greater symmetry, so that, to take but one example, there are considerably fewer belts overhead than in the photograph. The same freedom permitted the engraver to align machinery in perfect rows on both the right and the left side of the image, an effect apparently achieved by narrowing the passageway down the center of the room to the point where it would be dysfunctional if actually so arranged. The photographer, by comparison, had to emphasize one side of the room and included objects of interest to historians, such as the stools where the women sat during part of their work. This in turn suggests that the symmetry of the image—the women all stand—does not represent the normal appearance of the room, when the women could move to many positions, congregating briefly, sitting, and so on. Perhaps the most interesting change between the engraving and the photograph is the deletion of the well-dressed man. Such mediating figures, usually presented as visitors, were a staple of magazine illustration, representing the reader—the outsider looking in on the scene.

Their disappearance presaged the elimination of workers themselves from industrial landscapes in the following decade. Two images of the Schenectady Works Lightning Arrester Assembly Room underscore this change.[5] Numerous identical details prove that these were taken at the same time. The black box on the floor, lower center, and the handle of the vise are in the same positions, and close inspection will reveal many other such duplications. The obvious difference—the removal of the workers—is not the only one, however; the changes all have to do with lighting and suggest that the workerless image used a prolonged exposure time. Note the greater contrasts in the worker image, particularly the contrast between the face and the clothing of the man standing near the window. Overhead in this image a pipe has been clearly illuminated from the windows but will be hidden in the next exposure, while other details along the ceiling will become muted. Such evidence suggests that the workers were removed in order to permit a much longer exposure with small aperture, with the windows blocked much of the time.

In short photographers could achieve some of the even lighting effects of engravings if they removed workers and stopped all movement in the shop. But although these technical considerations may account for the increase in workerless industrial landscapes in early years, they cannot explain why management scarcely required images of workers at all by 1910, when they briefly all but disappeared as subjects. Indeed the numbers of workers in photographs declined at the same time that they became easier to include. The slower plates and poor indoor lighting of the 1890s would disappear in the next two decades. Nevertheless, between 1910 and World War I, management had little use for images of workers.

These two changes—the decline of group portraiture and the virtual elimination of workers from industrial landscapes—measure changes in the corporation. Managers, not photographers, ultimately chose which photographic genres could be used in the factory. For them the workers counted for less in 1910 than they had in 1895, while the means of production had become far more important. Comparing these early worker photographs with the machine's visualization in *General Electric*

Review in the same years, it is immediately clear that only the reification of machines passed over from engraving, with but minor changes in the following half-century. The photographic treatment of workers changed rapidly. Deleted from the workplace, visualized increasingly as large groups divided by skill (or lack of skill), by 1917 management needed to reconceive workers as a subject. That reconception was necessary also because management had transformed the productive system itself between 1890 and 1920. The old paternal relations between management and labor, based on personal ties, could no longer bind the corporation together.[6]

What had changed for the worker can be partially grasped in statistics. The General Electric employment rolls had grown from 6,000 in 1885 to 82,000 in 1920, with 16,000 workers in Schenectady alone. The turbines they manufactured had increased in horsepower during the same years by a factor of fifty. The number of General Electric product lines had jumped from 5 to 85.[7] The burgeoning work force that made these new products made management's role more important. Executives were no longer on the shop floor; they became more specialized and less capable of understanding the problems there. For the worker, the era when artisanal skills could be passed down from master to apprentice had all but disappeared. In the 1880s the electrical industry in particular had offered a refuge to skilled mechanics displaced from other trades, such as clock makers, machinists, tool makers, and other specialists.[8] By the 1920s the electrical industry needed fewer such workers as a percentage of its total work force. Instead there were new subdivisions in the jobs it offered employees, many requiring only minimal training. A few highly skilled workers were still vital to the implementation of any new manufacturing process or in retooling a shop. Indeed General Electric established a special apprentice course to ensure a steady supply of such workers. But proportionally they were a small part of the company work force compared to those in routinized and narrowly specialized jobs.

Management had subdivided labor, mechanized the work whenever possible, and introduced the assembly line. In the 1890s, for example, five men assembled meters at a single long bench.[9] Each understood how the mechanism worked and could put it together or take it apart. Thirty years later meters were assembled by a large force on a line with many work stations. Each person added but a single part, and none needed to understand how the meter worked. Manufacture of electric lights had changed similarly. Glass bulbs, once hand blown, were now machine made. Filaments, once produced and inserted individually, were now mass produced, and the manufacture of light bulbs could be accomplished almost entirely by young women who had little training.[10] Thus changes in scale implied new forms of production and an influx of semiskilled workers. Immigrants, as well as women, offered a source of inexpensive labor. By the 1920s thousands had come from Southern and Eastern Europe, particularly Italy and Poland. They swelled Schenectady's population from under 70,000 in 1890 to more than 130,000 by 1930, when their children made up more than half the school population.[11] These workers were largely unskilled, at times illiterate, and occasionally unable to speak English. They often had come to General Electric because a relative had promised to help them get employment in the plant, and in many cases they had come straight up the Hudson River from Ellis Island.

These immigrants offered cheap labor to the corporation, but they posed a problem as well. So heterogeneous a work force might prove ungovernable, especially when many came to the company without a tradition of factory work as part of their cultural heritage. As E. P. Thomson and Herbert Gutman have shown in their research, such workers did not readily adapt to industrial discipline.[12] Their inherited work habits were not compatible with monotonous assembly line work. They had been shaped by generations of artisanal and farm labor, characterized by alternating periods of intense work and casual leisure. To them work had a spontaneous rhythm, including breaks for relaxation, conversation, storytelling, and occasional festivities. Accustomed to agricultural and village life in their homelands, these immigrants were thrust into a work environment governed by the clock, where supervisors demanded an even work rate paced by an assembly line. They were to arrive at a specified hour, eat according to a timetable, and restrict their movements to a narrow work space. Accustomed to frequent holidays, such as saints' days and "St. Mondays," they were suddenly part of an unvarying routine, their actions monitored and controlled by supervisors whose language they understood imperfectly.

General Electric's efforts to discipline and control these

workers led to confrontations. The tensions of the workplace were magnified by the cultural conflict inherent in the situation, and workers began to identify themselves as a group sharply distinct from management. The workers in the 1890s at the Lynn plant had already mounted a successful strike for shorter hours, and in the next decade worker strength increased.[13] They joined unions, demanding better wages and more safety provisions. Although these were craft unions, organized according to skill, a larger vision of worker solidarity existed in the socialist movement.

While Eugene Debs championed the idea of one big union at the national level, in Schenectady itself a socialist movement focused on local, pragmatic issues. George Lunn, a charismatic clergyman turned politician, became Schenectady's mayor in 1911, sweeping the socialists into office. Essentially a reformer, Lunn initiated a variety of programs. He revalued property to favor workers instead of downtown businesses; he established free garbage collection; he built a large city park; he began an inspection program of meat and dairy products and ran a municipal farm to grow food for the needy; he set up free dental clinics in the city schools; and he used marriage license fees to sponsor free concerts.[14] Lunn had been elected by a coalition of middle- and working-class voters who wished to clean up the city government; he had not been elected on the basis of attacks on the free enterprise system or General Electric. But Lunn did support workers in their strike efforts, particularly in 1913, when he warned General Electric not to employ strikebreakers. Included in Lunn's City Council majority were several members of the International Association of Machinists.[15]

In addition to this alliance between reform socialism and craft unions, the International Workers of the World were active in Schenectady only one year after their founding in 1905 as they led a sit-down strike. An avowedly revolutionary organization, the Wobblies remained a force at General Electric until after World War I. They reached their greatest strength in 1918 when they helped to lead walkouts at the major General Electric plants: Lynn, Schenectady, Fort Wayne, Erie, and Pittsfield. A management representative believed that these actions were led by a combination of "the Socialists, the Russian Labor Union, the I.W.W., the anarchists, the Bolsheviks, and the more radical men in the established labor unions."[16] Yet despite this increase in worker political activity and militancy in the 1910s, during the 1920s worker unions virtually disappeared. The facile explanation for this reversal might seem to be a series of events such as the world war, the red scare and Palmer raids immediately afterward, and the general prosperity that followed. While these national and international events did affect General Electric, however, the company's own activities were more important factors in quieting labor unrest.

Initially it seemed as if the war might resolve the matter because it weakened the alliance between Mayor Lunn and the workers as the socialist movement fragmented at the time when strikes became illegal. It split into those who supported U.S. intervention and those who were neutral, viewing the war as inherently capitalistic. The federal government put Eugene Debs in jail and harassed other leaders.[17] In Schenectady Mayor Lunn, like many other pragmatic socialists, joined the Democratic party. He was elected to the New York State legislature.

The events of the war itself also made Americans suspicious of the foreign born. Most German newspapers were closed by government order during the war, as was the case in Schenectady. After the Russian Revolution, many Americans began to worry about the "communist menace" and about the susceptibility of foreign-born workers to the blandishments of Bolsheviks. Much has been written about the red scare of these years, but the less well-known labor reeducation programs affected far more individuals. These programs appeared in most parts of the nation at the end of the war, coming in with a wave of magazine articles that appeared in virtually every influential journal, including the *Nation*, the *Ladies Home Journal,* the *Literary Digest*, and the *Review of Reviews*.[18] Schenectady residents early began to organize, including General Electric managers, who developed an Americanization program shortly after a mass meeting in 1917 whipped up enthusiasm for classes.

The company worked with one of the recognized national leaders of the Americanization movement, Peter Roberts, from the YMCA. In 1920 Roberts published a book summarizing his experiences and recommending curricula and methods to employers. For him General Electric epitomized the ways in which a corporation could mobilize its native work force and build on the foreign workers' relationships with their employers to coerce participation. In Roberts's words:

One of the best examples is the General Electric plant in Schenectady. Here, under the leadership of an Americanization director . . . a splendid corps of teachers from among the employees have been trained to teach. If the work is done in the plant, it is very important that the director should come in personal contact with the foreign-speaking by personally calling on them in the place where they work. An accurate record of attendance should be kept and a regular system of follow-up work installed. We do not believe in compulsion, but moral suasion and sympathy.[19]

To men like Roberts, foreignness was an unfortunate condition, like alcoholism, to be treated with moral suasion and sympathy. Americanization was a cure. But to the immigrant worker at the plant approached by white-collar officials, foremen, and fellow workers, Americanization was a veiled order. In Schenectady hundreds enrolled.

To encourage similar programs, one General Electric vice-president helped form a national organization. E. W. Rice, perhaps not incidentally the half-brother of the head of the General Electric Publicity Department, was a founding member of the Inter-Racial Council in 1919, which sought to carry on the work started in 1917.[20] The council hoped to achieve the following results: "To stabilize industrial conditions. To apply American business methods to the foreign born press by building up an American advertising base under it. To reduce unrest and disorder through plant analyses. . . . To decrease radicalism through the issuances of information and counter education in the foreign language press dealing with attacks upon American institutions, law and order, and industry."[21]

Americanization was not an isolated program put into effect in the aftermath of World War I. Such efforts were parts of the larger movement of welfare capitalism, which had started well before 1914. Stuart Brandes has chronicled the movement as a whole from 1880 to 1940 in *American Welfare Capitalism*.[22] To cope with labor in these years, many corporations discovered it was in their own self-interest to create programs ranging from education and medical care to housing, profit sharing, safety, stock ownership plans, retirement benefits, and employee representation. Americanization was but one more corporate attempt to control workers' lives.

At General Electric Americanization had been preceded by an extensive safety program and an improved works' hospital.

After the beginning of World War I the company consolidated these services with a new sports program in the Welfare Department. The department also visited workers' homes when they failed to report for work two days in a row, and it encouraged compliance with the new prohibition laws. In short, the Welfare Department explicitly attempted to shape and control the lives of company employees. Charles M. Ripley explained and celebrated General Electric's welfare capitalism in two books the company issued in 1919, whose titles suggest the upbeat presentation: *Life in a Large Manufacturing Plant* and *The Romance of a Great Factory*.[23]

The beginnings of such programs antedated World War I but received a strong impulse from it. International Harvester, for example, began its work a decade before; Ford Motor Company and Goodyear Tire started at the same time as General Electric. In part the changing nature of the labor force accounts for these programs, coupled with corporate fear of unassimilated workers. But just as important was the opportunity created by the war itself. Not only did the government outlaw strikes, it also imposed a system of shop committees in many factories. These committees were to provide an orderly grievance process for individual complaints. They also participated in wage settlements and other negotiations. For this brief period the government effectively crushed the power of the unions and offered an organizational alternative. Such a shop committee system was imposed at the General Electric Lynn Works.[24] By permitting workers some participation, it hoped to make the company union appealing. After the end of the war the company tried to eliminate unions at its other plants as well. During the expansive years of the 1920s, the approach met with some success.

To work effectively, such welfare capitalist programs required effective communication. On one level an in-house magazine or newspaper simply announced sports events, classes, shop committee elections, and occasional recreation programs. But on another level magazines combated worker conceptions of the company and provided a positive vision of the factory. Periodicals carried stories such as "What Employee Publications Are Doing to Improve Industrial Relations." They could eliminate strife between capital and labor, encourage shared stock ownership programs, and create "in the employees generally a respect for the ideals and principles on which our country was founded."[25] Employee publications could combat foreign propaganda and reeducate the workers. Indeed Charles Steinmetz in one of the earliest *Works News* articles proclaimed that Bolshevism was an "industrial sickness" that could not spread in the United States because its workers had far more to lose than to gain from any revolution: "Most of the labor in Schenectady is Americanized labor, living according to American standards. They have seen labor conditions steadily improve."[26] Through many such articles companies replied to attacks on the capitalist system. As *Industrial Management* summarized, "The enemies of our government and our system of life are constantly at it hammering away with propaganda and literally tons of printed matter on socialism, communism, and other isms, in a ceaseless effort to destroy the present order of things. Employee publications are doing a great work in combating these enemies of our civilization."[27] Yet although this political explanation took precedence in the years after World War I, the reasons for company publications were far more complex, having to do not merely with political restructuring but with the redesign of the work force and its education to fit a social role different from the one it had played before.

The General Electric *Works News* exemplifies these company magazines and serves as a useful example of corporate ideology. Begun in 1917 at the same time as the Americanization program, it continued for two decades, with only a brief interruption in the 1930s. Blue-collar workers received it twice a month. For fifteen years its circulation was larger than that of the *New Republic* and the *Survey Graphic* combined. The *Works News* format was as advanced as those of its more famous contemporaries.[28] It carried many more illustrations than the *Survey Graphic* and was printed on much better paper than the *New Republic*. It did not address a general audience but rather was specially edited for each plant. The workers at West Lynn received a quite different publication from that distributed in Schenectady. Each factory magazine referred to only the activities at that site; reading the *Works News* one could find out nothing about blue-collar life in the company as a whole.[29] The larger company was represented by only a few managers, inventors, and generalized sales statistics. Thus, although multiple publications required many separate staffs and raised production costs, the corporation had an obvious interest in treating each factory as an autonomous world, building barriers between workers at different plants.

Subdivision of the work force was only a preparatory step; the publication sought to do far more with each audience created inside the corporation. Most obviously it promoted the new sports leagues, educational programs, and the company union. Workers might not necessarily be susceptible to written forms of persuasion, but the extensive photography that appeared in every issue of the magazine was more subtle. General Electric photographers developed several entirely new image classes to appear exclusively in the *Works News*. They did not directly address the issues of "socialism, communism, and other isms" or the transformation of the work process but rather projected a new conceptualization of workers.

The magazine cover carried a distinct class of images that had no precedent in the previous work of the General Electric photographers.[30] These were images of individual workers, shot from a distance of perhaps ten feet, showing the entire body of each. The worker usually stands, occupying the central space of the frame. He is not obviously posing but rather is immersed in an interesting, skilled job that is clearly visible and comprehensible. Only certain kinds of labor could be given photographic treatment; the majority of the jobs actually being done in 1919 did not qualify. Few pictures of assembly line work were suitable, for example, because the workers were seated and performed a single function. Their place of work could not be framed to create the sense of personal involvement with an important task, which was the central characteristic of all such cover photographs.

By comparison, the work of a skilled mechanic or a crane follower was ideal for such photographic treatment. The worker's individuality and the importance of the job could be made obvious at a single glance. The frame could include both the worker and the task, as the crane follower confidently stood beside the heavy load he guided through the plant, ensuring that it did not impede other work or endanger the lives of other employees. The woman operates a vertical milling machine in the Erie Railway Motor Department during World War I when fewer men were available for the job. In later years corporate captions became explicit: "Model G.E. switchboard being assembled to symbolically illustrate craftsmanship."[31]

These images expressed engagement, confidence, and skill. Repeated on the cover of almost every *Works News*, they insisted on a conception of labor that bore little relation to the actual work at General Electric for the majority of its employees. The reality of any particular cover in itself was undeniable, however, and since the editors did not insist on the universality of the working conditions or the kind of job depicted, the generalization remained implicit. Surprisingly inside the magazine were virtually no photographs of this type. Instead the articles and the images concentrated on a vision of the factory as a community where workers took vacations, played on sports teams, mutually contributed to pension plans, got married, held dances, celebrated Christmas, bought and sold household goods, and took a wide variety of evening courses. The photographs act as a series of visual proofs of the actuality of welfare capitalism.

Paradoxically, then, while the principal shared activity of the magazine's readers is work, the magazine's articles do not concern work, and the photographs do not depict it. Instead the workers play, as leisure replaces labor. By invading the terrain of sports, the company appropriated its employees' traditional pastimes. Organizing these into forms of competition through the formation of leagues and the award of trophies, General Electric made the casual play of bocci bowling or baseball into a test of quality. The industrial leagues not only organized play but transformed its meaning so that conflicts were displaced from the factory to a neutral arena. *Works News* carried pages of company sports news but nothing about the productive activities of the same athletes. The workers thereby were encouraged to find personal worth in what had been their pastimes.

Furthermore, sports photographs emphasized not the individual but the team. "Accounting Basketball Team" (1924) most closely resembles images made of women workers if compared to previous corporate work.[32] In each case the subjects are arranged in rows, facing the camera uniformly, holding similar postures, their hands on their knees or in their laps. The sports photographs record static moments of controlled repose, not the action of the playing field. They emphasize play, not playfulness. The status of athlete was important, but the process of playing the game was not. Free association also disappeared as the teams were organized by shop rather than voluntarily. Play thus reinforced the narrowest associations established in the factory rather than cutting across occupational lines.

Sports were the only vestige of individuating activities for workers. Here alone each had a name as part of a squad. Nameless and often faceless in the plant, on the sports field each had a democratic opportunity to excel. Sports were a safe democratization, leaving the industrial hierarchy intact. The players face the camera serenely, staring directly into the lens with confidence. Here they appear proud of their athletic regimentation; the image resembles those of high school yearbooks. As this comparison suggests, most players were young. When workers played, they were not only distracted from organization across shop lines, they were also focusing on physical skills and dexterity common only to youth. These same skills, however, were of little importance in the increasing specialization of the factory, where strength and agility counted for less than in previous eras. The team photograph enshrined what was less and less needed in the plant. Emphasizing physical prowess through the prestige of neat uniforms and the appeal of well-toned bodies, these were the most orderly of all worker photographs, using precisely arranged rows of players to provide an image of group achievement, a regimentation displaced from the workplace.

The unity of these images is quite different from that of the group photographs taken a generation earlier, which expressed a less routinized and more assertive solidarity in the workplace. A row of men or women in identical postures signified acquiescence to an unseen coach and thus to replication and human standardization. The uniform clothing offers one more confirmation of this same message, as does the frequent use of the company's monogram, stamped on the player's chest.

Two photographs—female workers wearing a company garment called "woman-alls" and a men's bowling team—typify this second class of *Works News* images.[33] These men and women are not working or producing; rather they are being produced. In this sense gender functions as a further indication of relative value. The sexes are separated in all photographs of this type. Women are usually presented from the side, emphasizing their breasts and hips. The uniform itself— the encompassing woman-alls—obscures the subtle differences among these female bodies. The resulting chorus line has been more completely standardized than those of the dance hall and burlesque show of the same era. The woman-alls are also a visual representation of the work experience. Their lack of pockets, belts, or frills that might be caught in the machinery both ensures safety and denies individuating signs of femininity or personal style. The uniform thus is a sign of corporate concern for the worker's safety but one submerged in the simultaneous cancellation of personality.

Sex does not so obviously affect the imaging of male workers, who face the camera frontally. Here the sign of pleasure is athletic. These men do not labor in a dirty shop; they enjoy bowling, wearing clean, neat uniforms. Like the machine photographed against a white background, they appear unrelated to any historical process. Bowling will remain the same sport regardless of changes in the economy or modernization in the shop. In both work and play, however, the notion of the team remains pivotal. Coordinated team play can be understood as a metaphor for group work. But in this displacement, the dynamic of production is reduced to the static re-creation of bowling and other sports, with their repetitive actions.

In such an image class the relation between sexuality or human reproduction and the corporation has been cancelled in several ways. Not only are the men and women separated initially; not only are they conceived as products of the company rather than as products of families; not only is their individuality erased by the standardization of the uniform and the repetition of poses; but equally important is the absence of any family photograph. From the *Works News* one could hardly discover that family groups worked together at General Electric. The biological family has been entirely effaced and replaced by a pseudo-community of the corporation, with its teams and groups. No hint of the complex human ties present in the work force, common to any factory town, may be found in any photographs until the 1940s. Only then does it emerge in the context of World War II: a photograph of five sisters of Polish descent all working to defeat Germany.[34] In this isolated exception the family can emerge as a meaningful unit because it is congruent with the needs of accelerated wartime production. But with few exceptions, the photographs of the *Works News* repeat the same implicit messages: workers are part of a community defined by the corporation; they are citizens of an industrial democracy with its workers' councils, athletic events, cooperative pension plans, and Christmas parties.

To make this industrial community complete, all of the workers must become full citizens. Those who cannot read and write the English language and who retain a foreign citizenship must become Americanized. In photographic terms, beginning in 1919, immigrants become a subject for the first time. Photographers began to take new kinds of images that captured at once their foreignness and their preparation for citizenship. "Boccie Bowling at Noon Recess" now became an "Americanization Activity," at once validating a pastime from the old country and enfolding it within the corporate family.[35] In posing for the photographer their leisure is not only interrupted; it becomes an initiatory activity. Compared to the heroic individuals on the cover of the *Works News* or the sportsmen in neat uniforms, these workers still pose like men of the 1890s. Americanization was to erase this anachronism so that they would no longer have unwashed faces, worn clothing, or shocks of unruly hair. Aside from the occasional sports images, which serve as transitions between ethnicity and the factory, the Americanization photographs form a sequence marking the stages of socialization. Early images show these immigrants seated in their shop after hours, studying English with a visibly American instructor, whose well-tailored jacket, clean shirt, and closely cropped hair immediately identify him as the model to be imitated. Over the course of a year in the *Works News*, photographs of such immigrants chart their transformation from outsiders to citizenship. They attend lectures and films; they engage in mock governments, playing the roles of congressmen, senators, and the president. They simulate the Teapot Dome investigation. They prepare for naturalization court. In the sequence of images the immigrants are transformed. Once seated, they are now erect. The worn clothing disappears, replaced by suits. Their bearing becomes more assured, and gradually they blend into a homogeneous mass, until the instructor cannot so easily be picked out from the group. By the end of the Americanization process they are no longer in the shop but in a courtroom, being sworn into the rights of citizens.[36]

The depiction of Americanization reveals the underlying thrust of the welfare program and the *Works News* itself: workers must conceive themselves as citizens, shifting identification from ethnicity and family to the corporation. Diversity must be eliminated, individuality suppressed. The *Works News* presented ideal workers assembled in identical groups, as citizens, athletes, or participants in leisure activities. Labor itself appeared only as a heroic individual effort, on the cover, while groups of people working never appeared. These two idealizations were complementary, projecting together a vision of integration. Socially the individual was integrated into a caring community of shared activities and benefits; on the job the worker was not alienated but immersed in satisfying production. The Americanization photographs can therefore be understood as only a special case of the general production of ideal workers. Just as advertising was to manufacture customers, internal publicity was to create producers.

There is no direct way of knowing how workers read *Works News* but only of how they responded to the programs the magazine promoted. Americanization was a qualified success, measured in the numbers of citizens produced. Although hundreds of Italians and Poles took the language courses, few completed the entire two-year program. Many Scots, Canadians, and Englishmen took the second-year courses in civics and citizenship, which also contained Swedes and Germans, who frequently spoke English well enough to be exempted from the first year's work.[37] These employees easily became Americanized, while the Southern and Eastern Europeans on the whole did not. Typically these students were married men, anxious to return to their families after a ten-hour day in the shop rather than remain for an hour of language instruction. At approximately thirty-five years old, they were past the age of easy language acquisition. In many cases their own children already were citizens by virtue of birth. To such immigrants the program probably appeared an unnecessary burden, and attendance figures bear out this interpretation.

Overall the company reported that participation averaged 75 percent.[38] After discounting for high attendance at rallies and movies and for the large number of English speakers in the second-year language program, it is clear that less than 75 percent attended the crucial language classes. Sections met only twice a week, meaning that the average worker attended the sessions only five or six times a month at best. The Americanization photographs therefore seem to be more the visualized ideal than the worker's own understanding of Americanization.

A more definite example of resistance to the messages of *Works News* was the reaction to the attempt to impose a company union. In 1922, after four years of intensive welfare capitalist publicity, General Electric submitted an industrial representation plan to the Schenectady plant. Management ran a series of articles favorable to the plan, charting the meetings held between corporate vice-presidents and labor.[39] After 84 employee representatives ratified the plan, it went to a larger group of 250, who also approved it. Yet despite this careful orchestration, the rank and file rejected the company union resoundingly by a vote of 5,707 to 3,549.[40] Many also abstained from voting. Overall less than 25 percent of the 16,000 workers favored the company plan in 1922. Two years later they did ratify a similar plan after another barrage of public relations in the *Works News*. By 1928 no unions were trying to organize General Electric, and the company victory over worker radicalism seemed complete.

In fact the corporation managed to impose its version of industrial reality only provisionally, through a great deal of repetition, at a time of general prosperity. Workers who had unionized and voted for a reform socialist mayor in one decade could not be converted into docile extensions of management's will in the next. Rather, the *Works News* was corporate ideology, a managerial dream about life in the factory.

After 1929 such an idealized workplace clearly did not exist, as workers lost their jobs or were demoted to part-time or less skilled work. The management-worker relationship could no longer be convincingly explained in terms of sports, concerts, educational programs, Christmas parties, and the like. Indeed management discontinued the *Works News* altogether in 1930 and brought back a scaled-down version the following year. The editors had no new formula for the magazine. They repeated the same image classes of photographs. One in particular, which made apparent sense in the previous decade, seemed particularly inappropriate in the depression. This was the personal portrait. The editors continued to sprinkle these through every issue, implicitly insisting that each individual's fate was distinct from that of the mass of workers. They repeatedly printed these images while never using those that showed groups working. This man has been promoted, has made a valuable suggestion, has taken an evening training course, has returned from the army, has taken a vacation. Such portraits and accompanying stories predominated at the end of each issue. Nowhere did the worker see his or her part in a larger effort or gain an understanding of the plant's organization, its marketing position, or the interconnections linking its many units. In the *Works News* the larger meanings of the plant had no place. It admitted only the discreet, individualized fact or the most general statistic.

Workers developed their own alternatives to company publications and social institutions. The union movement gathered force as the depression wore on. In the last years of the 1930s the company union lost membership to the Electrical Workers Union, and as Ronald Schatz has found through personal interviews, many of the union leaders were old stock, highly skilled individuals, not the Bolsheviks and immigrants whom management had feared would rise against them in the 1920s.[41] These leaders had begun to organize when they were forced to accept jobs at lower skill levels, and lower rates of pay, than they had achieved in the 1920s. Downward mobility shocked these men into action. The women leaders offered a somewhat different case; they had never been permitted to rise above the semi-skilled level in most cases. Among them the leaders were those who had worked the longest—usually single and divorced women—who had the most to lose. Like the men they over-turned the company union organization when it manifestly did not meet their economic needs. One can probably assume that company propaganda, no matter how intensive or sophis-ticated, could not have continued to convince workers to view their lives in the terms posed by the *Works News* in the 1920s.

Yet even within the context of the previous decade, that magazine had offered an internally flawed construction of indus-trial reality. Selected and edited as they were, the *Works News* photographs still contradicted themselves. By emphasizing workers as individuals immersed in nonalienated work, on its covers and in its many short biographical notes, the magazine offered an essentially nineteenth-century vision of workers and their place in a laissez-faire economic system. Yet its simultane-ous emphasis on nonwork activities offered quite a different vision: one of community achieved through the effacement of ethnic, familial, and class identity. At root these two versions of reality were at war. One expressed an individualistic, free market philosophy, the other, a paternalistic welfare capitalism inside a corporation. Neither of these sets of images depicted the actual work situation in the factory.

The *Works News* was not an internally coherent depiction of the world for reasons inherent in the communication situation itself. Consider the difference between the photograph made in 1876 at Menlo Park, of Edison and his fellow workmen, and those made at General Electric half a century later. In the first the same people are sending and receiving the message, and they are also its content. It was possible to include both labor and management in a single frame. None of these conditions obtained fifty years later. The *Works News* was a separate entity inside the corporation, with a staff permanently employed to send messages from management to the work force. Those who created the photographs were in turn subjugated to editors, who decided which images to print in the magazine, and they in turn responded to pressures inside the hierarchy of the corporation. Those ultimately responsible for the content of the magazine had no direct contact with those who would receive it. Even had a corporate vice-president wished to publish an in-house magazine that was completely accurate about blue-collar work, such a project would have failed because the executive's social reality differed from that of the worker. The manager paid the photographer's salary, who sought to please him, not the workers, and to validate his conception of the world, not theirs. Such mediated communication, regardless of intentions, necessarily leads to considerable distortion.

General Electric's management did not seek complete accuracy in the *Works News*. The magazine was designed to reeducate workers. The corporation published such a magazine, at considerable cost, only because it promised a clear return on its investment. By distracting and pacifying workers, *Works News* presumably reduced the number of strikes and work stoppages and increased profits as a result. The publication benefited the company, not the work force. Since such benefits are obvious enough, few have examined the precise nature of magazines such as *Works News* as parts of corporate communications.

To succeed, any communication requires that both sender and receiver share the same code. The corporation could find such mutually comprehensible codes in many arenas but chose to avoid the most obvious one, the workplace. The company instead evoked appealing images of work from the past. It offered sports as a substitute for work. It encouraged the idea of the corporation as a community. Indeed it substituted endlessly for the work process, drawing on many codes common in the larger culture. Thus the essential feature of corporate ideology for workers is not outright misrepresentation of the workplace but rather endless substitutions for and translations of work into other realms.

But in this continual substitution, contradictory stories and inconsistent images necessarily enter into the magazine. Some of these rewritings and revisualizations of the factory's meaning draw on the past; others move sideways into the present. As a result the magazine contains some nineteenth-century laissez-faire capitalist elements and others that come from its own contemporary period.

The argument here has two distinct strands. One has been the evolution of General Electric as a corporation, with changing needs for labor. It moved from small, artisanal beginnings to a large company with a great mass of unskilled labor. These changes in scale and in the labor force created conflict between management and labor and led the corporation to create a welfare department and a worker-oriented magazine. This story is familiar. The second strand of the argument is that these technological and economic changes also can be seen in the classes of photographs made at each stage. The early images of Menlo Park gave way to the assertive group portraits of workers, taken just before the turn of the century. These in turn disappeared completely. Fifteen years later company photographers invented a new series of image classes expressly for a new publication. Its images were a fundamentally different form of communication from those taken earlier. They systematically represented the corporation's meaning by focusing not on work but leisure, not on contemporary assembly lines but artisanal labor, not on the worker as part of a larger group but as an individual achieving autonomous success. All of these refocusings implicitly admitted the impossibility of reinterpreting work itself to the worker audience. Instead *Works News* displaced attention to points of agreement, such as America, or to neutral arenas, such as sports. Yet in this process of displacement, the corporation's ideology became inconsistent, incorporating elements from quite different symbolic systems, creating a mélange of contradictions. The company's own publication thus became an index of its ideological situation. It appeared at a moment of internal crisis in 1917 and continued only as long as it could contain that crisis through the projection of ideal communities of workers.

Photographically this containment took the form of several strategies of representation. The images of individualistic labor that graced the covers of *Works News* had a precedent in Lewis Hine's work for the Pittsburgh Survey conducted by the Russell Sage Foundation a decade earlier. Hine made similar photographs in the 1920s for such clients as the Pennsylvania Railroad and the Westinghouse Corporation. In his documentary work from this later period, gathered in *Men at Work*, he wrote, "The more machines we use the more do we need real men to make and direct them."[42] Hine depicted these "real men" most powerfully in images of the derrick men and skywalkers constructing the Empire State Building. General Electric photographers profitably adopted the style, similarly depicting men caught up in their difficult work. But in the corporation this style was but one of an ensemble of representational strategies that together defined the image world of the plant. The bulk of the photographs took the form of high school yearbook group portraiture, depicting evening classes, Christmas parties, sporting events, and the like. Only in the special case of the Americanization images can the photographers be said to have deployed a new strategy, particularly in the images taken of off-duty immigrant workers in language classes.[43] While the other Americanization images return to the yearbook style, here one glimpses the work environment, stripped of individualistic pretensions. And here alone, in the uncommitted eyes of these men and women, can we glimpse in a sideways glance, a blank stare, or a downcast look a legible resistance to corporate intentions. Yet such is the nature of photography, that it can recontain such gazes by placing them in a series of images that leads toward worker integration in a corporate community. Rather than being read as possible signs of protest, these faces become signs of foreignness that will be absorbed.

Edison and His Principal Assistants at Menlo Park, 1878

Punch and Die Department, 1901

Women Working in Wire and Cable Department, Building 14, c. 1900

Workers in Transformer Shop, c. 1893

View of the Main Floor of the Wire Insulating Department, 1888

Wire and Cable Department, Schenectady Works, c. 1895

Lightning Arrester Assembling Room (without workers), c. 1900

Lightning Arrester Assembling Room (with workers), c. 1900

Crane Follower in Motor Department, Directing Load to Be Raised, 1920

Bearing Shell Being Babbitted, 1929

Model G.E. Switchboard Being Assembled to Symbolically Illustrate
Craftsmanship

Women Operating Vertical Milling Machine in Railway Motor Department,
Erie Works, 1918

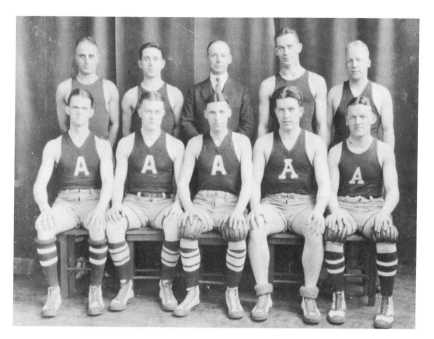

Accounting Basketball Team, 1924

Bowling Team, Bloomfield Works, 1925

Girls in Motor Department, Schenectady, Wearing Woman-alls, 1919

Americanization Activity, Boccie Bowling at Noon Recess, c. 1925

Americanization Class in English, Building 40, Teacher, H. Axford, 1924

Americanization Class in Civics, Preparing for Citizenship, 1924

Drama of U.S. Congress Enacted by Americanization Class in Civics, 1924

Americanization Class in Civics, Two Additional Students, 1927

6

Managers: The Corporation as Tribe

Berger and Luckmann make a central point in *The Social Construction of Reality* of the difference between the institutional order and the logical order superimposed on it by those who live within it. As they note, "Great care is required in any statements one makes about the 'logic' of institutions. The logic does not reside in the institutions . . . but in the way these are treated in reflection."[1] Or, as they conclude, "Reflective consciousness superimposes the quality of logic on the institutional order." In a small group, such as a family, it is not necessary to maintain this quality of logic through extensive written documents. Language and habit will serve. But in a large organization, especially one dispersed in space, the edifice of legitimations that gives a quality of logic to institutions can break down.

In the case of the workers at General Electric, the corporation created its own substitute for the edifice of worker perceptions. It displaced the labor unions' version of reality with a vision of the workers as separate communities. In this strategy the worker was to find institutional meaning not in work but in educational opportunities, sports, insurance plans, and other corporate programs. Community replaced class and family. *Works News* played a crucial role in stating and maintaining this logic of factory life.

The definition of reality offered by *Works News* was inadequate, however, for a managerial audience. Both its content and its structure were inappropriate for white-collar personnel. *Works News* distracted workers. It told them to find meaning in nonwork activities, and it presented a noncompetitive image of conformity and community. Such values were unsuitable for the managers, who had to strive and compete. Similarly, although it sufficed for workers to know a single task and do it well, managers needed to understand the company beyond one department.

The general state of management as a profession in the early twentieth century was far different from that of medicine, law, or engineering. To enter those fields, one needed a specific educational training, which had been standardized. Each field had its own journals, professional associations, and other forms of institutionalization. By comparison managers were a disparate lot, drawn from many backgrounds, with few common experiences as a group. The organization of large enterprises in 1920 was still decidedly mixed, with some firms controlled by family groups, others overseen by financiers, and only a few of the largest enterprises run by managers. The profession of management was only emerging, most significantly in the creation of business schools. The first of these, the Wharton School at the University of Pennsylvania, was founded in 1881. Its courses "included little more than commercial accounting and law," however, and the modern form of business education, using the case method and emphasizing managerial techniques rather than methods drawn from other fields, dates from the early twentieth century and is correctly associated with the Harvard Business School, which opened in 1908.[2]

By the 1920s all the marks of professionalism—national societies, university degrees, and specialized journals—had appeared, but the transformation had only begun. The new "business school graduates [were] still in the lower ranks." General Electric therefore faced a particularly difficult problem of unifying its managers, whose backgrounds included study at the new business schools, engineering, the company's well-known test course, law, sales experience in the field, German technical universities, and the proverbial school of experience.[3]

In later decades employees came from relatively uniform backgrounds and arrived at the company as professionals. But in the 1920s there were virtually no professional managers; moreover, "Engineers and salesmen considered each other separate races of people. Neither knew nor cared what the other fellow was doing."[4] Managers doing quite similar work in theory often proceeded in quite different ways.

To complicate the matter, General Electric was diversifying its product lines at a rapid rate, moving particularly into the consumer sector. The company was becoming a mass marketer to a greater extent than in its first twenty-five years, and it was con-fronting new kinds of sales and distribution problems. General Electric was also becoming even less centralized than it had been in the 1890s, acquiring new plants in Pittsfield, Bridgeport, and Philadelphia. In brief the company had taken on new functions, expanded to distant locations, and determined to make new products. And it had to make these changes with a heterogeneous group of managers.

There was little institutional cohesion; executives and middle managers shared no common vision of the corporation. Each individual knew only a small part of it, and there were few opportunities to pool information and insights. Yet at this time the complexity of management was increasing, not only because of the company's expansion into new markets and its geographical dispersion but because decision making was being transferred from the shop floor to the executive suite. As Chandler notes:

In production, the first modern managers came in those industries and enterprises where technology permitted several processes of production to be carried on within a single factory or works (that is, internalized). In those industries, output soared as energy was used more intensively and as machinery, plant design, and administrative procedures were improved. As the number of workers required for a given unit of output declined, the number of managers needed to supervise these flows increased. Mass production factories became manager intensive.[5]

At General Electric the changes that decreased worker autonomy necessarily increased managerial interdependence. Greater company control over workers could be achieved only through a unified system of administration.

The problem of management inverted the problem posed by labor. Where there had been a danger of too much solidarity, here was the danger of disintegration. Where it had been expeditious to encourage workers in myopic concerns, managers required a broad vision of the company. Rather than distract potential leaders, the problem became one of finding leaders. Rather than impose routines and disciplines as a logical and natural part of the daily round, with managers it was vital to disrupt absorption in specialized tasks. General Electric required unifying institutions that would give managers a common experience, and it developed two: a summer camp and a publication, the *Monogram*. The magazine articulated a conception of the company that managers periodically could act out on corporate holiday at the symbolically named Association Island.

General Electric owned the island, located on Lake Ontario, near the St. Lawrence River. For approximately fifteen years before 1922, when General Electric first used it, NELA had sponsored camps there each summer to bring managers from its many affiliated companies into personal contact. In 1922 five new camp meetings were held: "one for each of the major departments of engineering, manufacturing, commercial work, and merchandising, and a general camp for men drawn from all departments."[6] With the original camp for lighting managers, there were six in 1922. Camps for each of five corporation divisions were of equal importance; Camp General had more prestige. Attendance at any of them was a privilege for a select few, but the most coveted invitations were those to the only camp where important men came from every part of the company. No women were invited. The camps had the same male aura that pervades college fraternities, exclusive men's social clubs, the Masons, and other groups such as the Bohemian Grove, which still flourishes in California.[7] Like these institutions, the camps at Association Island isolated a group of educated, upwardly mobile and/or upper-class men. The privacy of these groups was emphasized by the location of their retreat: an island on the border between Canada and the United States. The importance of the camps to professional advancement could scarcely be doubted. Only there could a young executive meet the highest officers of the corporation.

At the most obvious level, these camps served as a system of recruitment into the upper echelons of the company. Younger executives could be observed there intensively for five days. Their behavior in sporting events, casual discussions, and the ceremonies of camp life, gave officers of the company more insight into their strengths and weaknesses. This function of the camps clearly was understood; management kept a file listing the names of promising young men, keeping track of their progress and achievements in the company. Everyone in the corporation knew that some younger white-collar men were secretly designated PYMs. The only way to know who was on or off the list lay in the invitations to Camp General and the departmental camps.

For those invited their precise status remained a mystery. Kurt Vonnegut parodied these camps in *Player Piano*, based in part on his years as a General Electric employee. When his principal character arrives at the Meadows, he recalls how many company men "were forever seeing omens" in the smallest incidents, "omens in a superior's handshake, in the misspelling of a name in an official document, in the seating arrangement of a banquet table, in a superior's asking for or offering a cigarette."[8] His world is thereby mystified as trivia and minor social encounters become an elaborate sign system. The best way for the candidate to succeed, therefore, is to be an exemplary team member, cultivating all opportunities to shine in the games, skits, and sports competitions at the camp.

In addition to this recruitment function, the camps had two latent functions as well: they established a set of criteria that transcended the specific work of an individual seeking advancement and created a sense of the corporation as a whole beyond its existence at particular sites. All three functions were embodied in the hierarchy, so clearly evident, which could be likened to a series of concentric circles. At the center of the hierarchy stood those invited to Camp General year after year, including famous scientists, such as Irving Langmuir and William D. Coolidge, the chief officers of the corporation, and a few outside celebrities. For example, in 1930 the following also came to Camp General: Bruce Barton, New York advertiser and General Electric adviser; Rear Admiral Richard E. Byrd, then the most famous American explorer; Adolph S. Ochs, publisher of the *New York Times*; John H. Trumbell, the governor of Connecticut; and the presidents and vice-presidents of several companies.[9] Since the camp could accommodate only 200 persons, the number of young, still unknown executives included was quite limited.

Many of those disappointed could be invited to one of the departmental camps, the second ring in the circle of power. Initially there were only five such camps, but by 1930 they had expanded to ten so Association Island was in constant use through the summer months.[10] The camps proved popular, and pressure mounted to include as many executives as possible. With ten camps total attendance could reach 2,000 in a summer. Since some officials went to several, however, the actual number of persons attending was smaller.

At the periphery of corporate life were managers not invited to any camp, no matter what their official title. Although some had to stay at their jobs "minding the store," few did so willingly. The net effect of the institution of summer camps was not only to recruit a few promising men into the highest levels of management but also to give many more the illusion that they might be on the ladder to success, even if they were excluded in a given year. Anyone might be a promising young man in disguise, and so long as one received an occasional invitation to the summer camps, there was hope for advancement. The institution excited expectations and linked managers to the corporation.

If the structure of the camps encouraged competition and ambition, their content stressed community and cooperation. The talks and more informal discussions focused on the linkages between various departments and levels of management. For example, in 1929, Camp Service held a number of meetings in addition to general sessions: "Special meetings were held by the following groups: service shops; Works production, Works shippers, Warehouse superintendents, Contract Service Department representatives; General Office and Works engineers; Commercial Service and Order Service; Order Manual."[11] To dramatize Camp Service's theme, some of the employees staged a skit entitled "Service, from 'As You Like It.'" Such short plays were a feature of every Association Island camp. Camp Commercial saw one on market analysis in 1929, and the following year Camp Refrigeration produced a two-act play "dramatizing the need for organization on the part of distributors. Discussion followed."[12] In these and other ways the camps emphasized cooperation, although those attending were competing to rise higher in the company.

Camp life as a whole overcame this contradiction by upsetting all of the normal routines of its managers. Usually confined to their desks, at Association Island they spent virtually all of their time outdoors for four days and nights. They wore sports clothing instead of business suits. They held open-ended discussions instead of making decisions. Divisions based on work were abolished, replaced by divisions based on cabin assignments and athletic teams. Instead of work, games. Instead of the family, manly camaraderie. Cut off from the rest of the world on an island, a privileged few inverted the corporation's values and lived according to a special set of rules.

The parallels to a secret society in a so-called primitive culture are many. The camps were yearly midsummer festivities of a selected and secret society and included the initiation of new members. All camps had ceremonial regularities. Four elements recurred each year. First, each camp began with a parade of all those attending. Positions in the parade were carefully determined. For example, in 1930 those who "had achieved the best sales records were given special privileges at Camp Refrigeration IV, and, in addition, headed the parade which always is an opening ceremony."[13] Such men resemble the braves of an Indian tribe who lead a dance because of their victory in battle or the hunt. In other camps the determination of a rank order for the parade might be based on such factors as years of attendance at the camp or seniority in the company, but it usually was not a simple transcription of rank. The parade, after a long trip north and a boat ride to the island, marked the division between the daily routine and the inversion of that routine in the camp. It formalized the passage from one order to another, as the men wore informal clothing and marched in an order that, like their selection for the camp itself, had been determined by high-level company officials.

One of these officers appeared at each camp, and such a presence itself overturned the employee's everyday experience that the president, the chairman of the board, and other top managers were aloof and distant. One of these figures addressed each camp. For example, "On the island . . . Swope developed his own special brand of eloquence. He would give a short summary of what he considered important company operations. This would be replete with figures." Afterward he answered questions from the floor on any aspect of the business: "In rapid, animated but often incomplete sentences he would explain policy or practice on prices, plant conversion, research, selling, advertising, labor, salaries, bonuses, vacations, new products, anything. . . . Swope keenly enjoyed pitting his prodigious memory and the quickness of his perceptions against all comers."[14] The give-and-take of such question and answer sessions was crucial. These interchanges were impossible during the rest of the year. They gave each executive a chance to be noticed but at the price of a public test of quickness and intelligence with the president. Just as important the executive's performance proved he deserved loyalty and respect. It demonstrated his right to confer distinction on others.

A third feature of each camp consisted of symbolic enactments at public ceremonies. Members wore special costumes appropriate to their roles in these events—for example, dressed as lumberjacks holding white sacks. These costumes were justified on the island where the company suspended the normal rules of behavior. The men symbolically represented the linkage among the five departments of the company. Each held a ten foot pole topped by a pennant. The man carrying research had a banner proclaiming "clear thinking," the man of sales carried one proclaiming "vision," and so forth. At another camp two men wore white robes and held placards that read "Virgins 99 44/100% pure" and "Lonesome Eunuchs." At another three dressed like Roman soldiers, brandishing spears as they surrounded a podium.[15] Since only photographs kept in the company archives survive of these events, the specific content of the various rites cannot be analyzed. But they clearly united executives through the performance of actions that could not be fully reported outside Association Island. The secrecy was ensured in part by the adolescent and absurd nature of these activities. The camps became a sanctuary where regression to premarital male bonding was actively encouraged.

The symbol at these camps for the corporation as a whole was a giant elm tree that stood near the water's edge. Each camp held a solemn ceremony around the tree at dusk on one of the last nights.[16] The giant elm was illuminated to stand out against the gathering darkness, and an older member of the company briefly addressed the camp members. The choice of the tree as a symbol is hardly unique to General Electric. Societies in widely scattered parts of the world have used a pole or a tree to represent the connection between heaven and earth, including the American Sioux Indians. And as at General Electric's camps, ceremonies held around such a tree or pole usually occurred during the summer months, often during the solstice.[17]

Since no direct observations can be made of the Association Island camps, their comparability to events studied by anthropologists cannot be determined in detail. But at a general level Victor Turner's characterization of liminal states as temporary psychological phenomena that occur in ritual processes seems to fit the General Electric case. Turner examines rites that offer a blend of "lowliness and sacredness, of homogeneity and comradeship" to their participants. These rites provide a vitally important counterpoint to experience in the hierarchical world of everyday life. Turner's description appears almost to be a gloss on the Association Island meetings: "We are presented, in such rites, with a 'moment in and out of time,' and in and out of secular social structure, which reveals, however fleetingly, some recognition . . . of a generalized social bond that has ceased to be and has simultaneously yet to be fragmented into a multiplicity of structural ties." That is, the generalized social bond that once connected all executives together in the early years of the company's history and has ceased to be is temporarily recreated at the summer camps. Afterward the fragmentation will reoccur each year, but the edifice of legitimations—the executive's perception of the corporation as a social unit—will have been reestablished. The existence of the Association Island camps inside the corporation exemplifies Turner's observations.

It is as though there are here two major "models" for human interrelatedness, juxtaposed and alternating. The first is of society as a structured, differentiated, and often hierarchical system of politico-legal-economic positions, with many types of evaluation separating men in terms of "more" or "less." The second, which emerges recognizably in the liminal period, is of society as an unstructured or rudimentarily structured and relatively undifferentiated *comunitas*, community, or even communion of equal individuals who submit together to the general authority of the ritual elders.[18]

General Electric was nothing if not a hierarchical system of politico-legal-economic positions in which many forms of evaluation divided people from one another. The camps at Association Island provided a necessary ritual reintegration. Turner concludes that social life has a dialectical character, moving between these two states, each of which requires the other in order to achieve full definition and meaning. By providing such a· dialectic between highly structured, hierarchical managerial work and the minimally organized retreat at the island, General Electric united an otherwise disparate corps of managers. Through a common experience of the *comunitas* at Association Island and its contrast to the everyday life of the corporation, they became initiates into a secret society, individuals marked by and merged into the company.

The camps at Association Island served two apparently

contradictory functions. They united executives from many branches of the organization, but they also divided the company into three concentric groups, the innermost being those invited to Camp General. To those in the outer two groups, particularly those not invited to any camp, the unrelieved experience of the hierarchical corporation plus their exclusion from the retreat heightened competitive tension. The fact of a secret, but not its contents, had been communicated to them.[19] The existence of antistructure thus highlighted the structure of the company as a whole.

The passage from overt competition at the factory to Association Island required that an executive forcibly relax. Its rites emphasized cooperation and teamwork, laughter and self-deprecation, not individual striving for success. Thus if the creation of the camps increased the hierarchical tension in the company, the experience itself denied and recontained that fact through egalitarian rites. The camps gave General Electric's corporate life a dialectical quality and erected a nonmaterial reward as the sign of executive success. They made the company appear to be more than a mere business. For managers it had become a tribe.

The retreat at Association Island established a bond among executives, but a single week's activities could not suffice for the whole year. The *Monogram*, a monthly magazine sent to managers, began publication in the same year the camps began.[20] Both institutions cut across divisional and bureaucratic lines, reaching and attempting to unite all the executives in General Electric. The magazine's name referred to the corporate symbol, not to a specific class of employees or to a specific location. The stories it carried dealt with a much wider range of topics than any other company publication, thereby seeking to acquaint executives with every aspect of the business. The second issue, for example, covered a wide range of topics: a review of two of the past summer's camps, district engineering problems, warehouse service, electric ship propulsion, a prize-winning electric railway on Boston's North Shore, "Who's Who in General Electric" (a recurring feature spotlighting a few individuals each month), company advances in radio, a $140,000 gift to Japan, important new orders received, brief notes on company activities, and a few press clippings. In addition there was a poem on the district engineer.[21] The issue as a whole contained forty 7 × 10 pages, profusely illustrated. Most issues averaged at least one photograph per page. The typical article covered only two or three pages, with one-third to half the space given to photographs. Such stories could not cover any subject in depth but rather served to give a rapid impression of corporate activities.

The *Monogram*, in hindsight, clearly proved complementary to the camps on Association Island. But at the time of the first issue in October 1922, the editors appeared to believe that "it is expected this publication will be interesting and instructive to our entire organization" and that it would prove to be "especially so to the sales organization. It will contain descriptions of large orders, particularly orders covering materials of new or novel nature, of changes or improvements in our organization and methods, and, in general, any information that will be of benefit to the sales force."[22] The editors requested that all members of the organization contribute ideas and articles. In fact, however, a regular staff in the Publicity Department wrote virtually all of the magazine. As early as the second issue the emphasis on salesmen in the audience began to wane. The *Monogram* soon became the principal channel of communication between upper and middle management. As with *Works News*, that communication worked almost entirely in one direction, from the top down.

The photographs employed in each were quite different, however. Examination of eight randomly selected issues of the *Monogram* from 1924 to 1930, when the program of welfare capitalism was fully implemented, reveals no images of Americanization activities, of workers performing skilled autonomous tasks, or of their sports teams.[23] Labor appears only as part of a vast interior landscape. The most common landscapes of the factory after 1920 excluded workers completely. The *Monogram* almost always contained several of these, and they constituted 10 percent of the photographs in an average issue.[24] The photographers composed these images to emphasize a repetitive order. They used long aisles, regularities in the ceiling, or a recurring element of the machinery to create coherence, perspective, and order in a space that might easily have been photographed as incoherent. Their work thus created a metaphor for managerial control through design. Often the photographers turned technical limitations into part of the vocabulary of control. None of these industrial perspectives leads to a window, for purely technical reasons, because the contrast would be too strong. The vistas are therefore almost always sealed off by walls, creating a representation of containment. By placing the camera near a door or window and gazing down a long, open aisle, the photographer thus made more than an image free from overexposure; he transformed factory space into an orderly realm where the manager's rationality was concretized.[25]

The contrast between such images and the typical product photograph in the *General Electric Review* suggests the differences between technical and managerial values. The engineers saw individual machines that had been invented, installed, and used; managers saw complex spaces under control. Engineers saw an elimination of shadow, singularity, and results, managers a rich interplay of light and shadow, multiplicity, and process. For engineers workers occasionally function as a means of measurement; for managers workers appear only incidentally, in the distance. They are bent over their tasks, oblivious to the camera, and the framing may lop off a head or an arm. They are unconscious of the camera. Only the foreman is perpetually aware of it, looking solemnly up to meet its gaze. Such images represent a hierarchical relationship: manager, foreman, worker.[26] Managers are only implicitly present, above the image, communicating with a designated representative, not with the workers themselves.

Appropriately the most common class of photograph in the *Monogram* permits this manager to stare back at a fellow executive's portrait—in effect, to look at himself. The format of these images contained their content. They remained virtually unchanged from shortly after the company began in the 1890s for half a century. Only head and shoulders were taken, with a spot of light behind the head to emphasize its centrality.[27] A dark screen fills the rest of the frame, removing the subject from any context. There were almost no frontal views. Head canted slightly to one side, the executive's eyes gazed into the infinite space implied by the lack of a surrounding context. The camera looks slightly up at each face, and darkroom retouchers removed its blemishes. The manager is olympian, outside petty concerns. He labors with his mind; the body does not count. He deserves the special attention of a close-up, yet he maintains the reserve of a captain of industry, even from an intimate distance. These photographs can be reproduced in virtually any size and the subjects will retain their dignity. Usually, however, they fill at least one-quarter of a page (see plate facing p. 71).

The full meaning of such images emerges in contrast to those of workers. A series of oppositions defines their ideological meaning within the corporation. The executive is singular; workers are plural. One works with his mind, the other with his hands and body. One is lifted to olympian status, the other is incidental. The executive requires only one kind of picture for full corporate definition, and in that image he never smiles or shows emotion. The worker is variously defined as a corporate product, an exemplary producer, part of a community, or part of the industrial landscape. The worker's mood therefore may vary among solidarity, stoicism, or blank inscrutability. In all of these classifications the worker wears exemplary clothing that expresses his position. The executive always wears coat and tie. But these codes of dress are supplementary (part of a second-ary coding) when compared to the coding of photographic technique. Relative distance from the camera expresses the im-portance of each: the worker is literally kept away and seen from a distance. The inclusion of his entire body means that compared to the executive he is not an intimate but a stranger. The executive glance is softer, less directed at the camera. He appears pensive; the worker stares directly down the lens, con-fronting the photographer. Secondary coding may reinforce this stare: workers often are dirty, wear clothing that is obvi-ously foreign, stand uncomfortably, or give other signs of otherness.[28]

As an unintended result of these codings images of the work-ers are often much stronger and make a more lasting impres-sion than do those of their managers. This is due not only to the play of secondary elements in the composition of the image, such as the greater variety in backgrounds, dress, and the like, but, more important, develops from the direct contact between their eyes and the lens. Unlike the executive who came to a studio to have his image made, the worker was caught in midst of the daily round, and his face carries all the traces of im-mediate experience.

The contrast between worker and manager images does not emerge from the *Monogram*. There virtually no workers ap-pear, and the factory is an empty industrial landscape waiting to be directed and controlled. But the magazine required some equivalent of production, some personalized vision of work, and the inventor filled this role. In almost every instance the inventor appears in a format quite unlike that used for the executive. The camera retreats slightly to show him from the waist up. He is usually hunched in conversation or at work at a site immediately identifiable as a laboratory. His hands are always visible and usually active—holding or manipulating. He usually sits, surrounded by the devices of his trade. Often he ponders a problem or the prototype of a new machine. His slightly averted eyes do not stare into infinite executive space but at a concrete mystery, the new thing he has fabricated.

Often, as in "Dr. Whitney in His Laboratory Listening to Electrons," the inventor is immersed in work, oblivious to the camera. His stance and the laboratory environment tell the viewer that here is a historical personage. The inventor creates history, producing it in bursts of energy. For him there is a past of achievement, a present labor, and the hint of future, inconceivable creations that will come from penetrating the secrets of lightning or the electron. Such infinite possibilities represent the only history the corporation celebrates.

General Electric's photographers did not themselves begin the portrayal of scientists and inventors. John Singleton Copley's *Portrait of Paul Revere* (c. 1770) can be seen as a prototype of the inventor image. Revere sits at a table, holding in his left hand one of his own creations, a silver teapot, with a few tools nearby, while he ponders putting the finishing touches on it. But unlike the preoccupied inventor, Revere's gaze falls on us as well so that the work of being a silversmith forms the linkage between himself and the world. Revere is portrayed as a person far more than as a human type. A similar direct engagement between subject and viewer can be found in a characteristic French portrait from the same period, Jean François-Gilles Colson's painting of the chemist and mineralogist, *Balthazar Sage*. As in the later General Electric inventor portraits, Sage appears in his study, sitting at a table, visible from the waist up. Around him are the many tools of his profession, such as glass vials and bottles, while behind his head beakers and other apparatus are shelved in neat rows. But again like Revere, the scientist gives his direction both to his work—through a gesture with his left hand—and to the viewer beyond the frame of the painting. What distinguishes the corporate image of the scientist, then, is not the setting, the informality of the pose, or the emphasis on science and work; rather it is the depiction of a self-absorption that excludes the beholder. A Steinmetz or an Edison communes not with us but with the infinite world of scientific mysteries. Such genius cannot be grasped in a single portrait.

The inventor is a multifaceted subject. Charles Steinmetz, to take the most prominent example (plates 42–45), was not exhausted as a subject in a single image. He alone is free to appear fragile, temporary, whimsical, casual, bemused. The profusion of images itself shows his fecundity, variety, and genius. For him no sure line divides work from play. He is the ultimate unalienated worker who controls the means of production and decides what to produce. He therefore is tireless and works for pleasure. Steinmetz and Edison work in the laboratory, at home, on vacation, at night—perpetually.[29]

The inventor is a perfect vehicle for the corporation. His myriad images can adorn all company publications. Within the plant he represents productivity fully integrated with the needs of capital. Every worker benefits from his labor, and anyone who can so help the corporation implicitly can rise to his status. The repetition of his face thereby substitutes for the worker's own face; in the inventor they must learn to see themselves.

Outside the plant the inventor represents the harmonious development and the unassailable virtue of the corporation. He is the emblem of progress, the sign of civic virtue, and the proof of every argument. The individual executive in comparison hardly exists as a personality. Executives endlessly repeat the same pose, with different faces. Inventors strike many poses, while the face itself becomes a hallmark. Such faces prove useful half a century after their death, while the manager is quickly forgotten—a price paid for the olympian pose that first released him from history. The corporation has a myriad executives; a sign of efficiency must be their continual production. Inventors are one of a kind, and therefore they alone can stand for the company's past and promise.

Photographs of executives, inventors, and the unpeopled industrial landscape together accounted for more than half the images in the *Monogram*. The remainder were quite diverse in keeping with the wide range of topics covered in the magazine's articles. But even this diversity proves more a matter of subject and location than style. On a general level the photographs concern products recently put in service, buildings, and exhibitions, suggested in sample images of Barcelona and São Paulo. Only the *Monogram* provided its audience with such continual reminders of General Electric's activities outside the factory. But the majority of these images depicted few people. The product, building, or fair, while clearly in the world, does not take on meaning in terms of human contact or use. Rather these photographs depict a society dominated by property relations. As in the industrial landscapes, when people appear they are either incidental or demonstrate the primacy of the machine. Photographs of buildings virtually never included passers-by, and those of fairgrounds were taken before or after visiting hours. The overall impression these pictures make in the *Monogram* is that of a worldwide dispersion of General Electric products. The magazine depicts a global penetration of the environment without noting the impact of electrification on people.

The *Monogram* reinforced the separation of managers from society and from the General Electric work force, institutionalized in the isolation of Association Island. The imagery of the magazine reiterates executive dominance and control not over people but over space. Whether inside or outside the plant, the corporation is its machinery, its products, its buildings. The executives stand outside the frames of these landscapes as isolated figures.

The only recurring image of human community in the magazine, as a result, is that of the camps of Association Island. Stories and images remind the reader of either the previous or the coming summer and emphasize group activities. Many articles in the magazine had first been given as talks at Association Island. The island's importance can be seen as well in the use of imagery on the cover. The November 1923 *Monogram* cover showed the company's tree silhouetted against the sky at sunset.[30] Similarly every year at least one cover would remind the executive reader of the summer camps.

The Association Island photographs often make little sense to an outsider. They do not always reveal the identities of the people depicted or fully explain the activities going on in the picture. The images are intentionally solipsistic. They send a message only to those who already have the information, reminding the uninitiated that some executives are party to secrets. These photographs activate the legitimations that superimpose the quality of logic on the life of the corporation.

No individual is ever alone in photographs from the site. The island represents the only vision of human community in the *Monogram*, which otherwise presents an impersonal world where the managers dominate unseen workers and consumers. The executives are a privileged class. They are not competitors in an enormous corporate bureaucracy but a closely knit fraternity.

Camp General does not appear in the guise of a small, private world, however, but rather as an opening into the highest echelons of American life. Images of famous visitors with corporate officials cement the national importance of Association Island. The visitors' casual attire and informal gestures suggest an easy intimacy. Here alone do executives have arms and legs, play games, and express themselves. The island emerges as a realm of privacy. Appropriately the photographs themselves have a snapshot quality and alone in the entire collection were made with a hand-held camera with $4' \times 5'$ negatives. With the smaller camera the photographer had more mobility, taking less time to prepare each shot.

Formality returned, however, in images of the same individuals taken away from the island. They depict famous visitors to the General Electric plants and laboratories, almost invariably joined by a corporate official. The photographs are much like typical tourist photographs: a small group stands on the steps of a building or before a machine, immobile and self-consciously presented to the camera. But these tourists are themselves the sights.[31] While ordinarily the tourist wants to be associated with the site, here the industrial site aspires to be identified with the tourist. To achieve this identity, suitable General Electric personnel must appear in the picture. Portraits of these famous visitors alone would necessarily reduce the corporation to background; the linkage would not be made.

These photographs differ from the others because they are formal portraits of groups. The camera must be farther away than in individual portraits, and the symmetry of the face must be replaced by a symmetrical arrangement of bodies. The effect is quite formal, with the faces unexpressive. The placement of the bodies, the camera's upward-looking angle, and respectful distance leave no doubt that these are beings superior to the machinery and the products of the corporation.[32] In these photographs and in those at Association Island, the corporation is linked to the human community. It is not a world of ordinary men and women or of petty material interests but one of great minds: serious, inventive, entrepreneurial. Beyond the company lies the world of celebrities. The two are contiguous, and the island is their common ground.

Together the camps at Association Island and the *Monogram* served the same end of integration. The camps provided a ritual release from the ordinary, hierarchical world and served as a principal path to success. The magazine reasserted the hierarchy of the plant and gave managers a clear sense of their position in that hierarchy. It educated them about the company's diverse functions and the wide dispersion of its products. The photographs in the *Monogram* literally showed managers their roles: coordinators of space, organizers of equipment, decision makers whose orders would be carried to workers through intermediaries. The manager appeared only in etherialized standardization, in portraits, or in conjunction with celebrities from afar. He was not part of the mass of workers. His counterparts were in other factories, where he might be transferred. Both the magazine and Association Island encouraged him to locate the company not in the immediate world of the office but in a more abstract realm, like that implied in the blank backdrop to a personal portrait. His General Electric existed not in one place but would be anywhere the company might send him. His loyalty was to this generalized possibility, not to a single site. His advancement promised disruption and separations. Distancing made a manager professional.

The managers' image world diverged sharply from that of the engineers. The *General Electric Review* avoided the social and economic realms entirely, depicting the corporation solely in terms of isolated machines, graphs, charts, and equations. Its images almost never contained individuals; they never showed an ongoing process. In contrast the *Monogram* stressed the socioeconomic realm, providing managers with an overview of corporate activities. Yet it did not depict the factory in terms of human transactions but rather as a series of abstract spaces to be controlled from above. The production process itself was deemphasized in favor of a static representation of industrial landscapes. In these the factories' architectural design becomes a metaphor for rational organization, while workers appear as an undifferentiated mass, if they appear at all. The apotheosis of this olympian vision was the aerial photograph, which presented the factory as a geometrical order. The Schenectady Works (plate 48) becomes an abstract realm of productivity between the town and the country. Spatial rather than human relationships express the plant's meaning just as they did in interior landscapes.[33]

The only human community necessarily lay outside the factory gates, at Association Island. In that apparently natural space, a pastoral antithesis to the industrial landscape, the company could represent itself as a series of interlocking clans, each called to an annual camp, where its warriors could be sifted to find the next leaders. Except for that private community on the St. Lawrence River, the manager had no other allegiance. The *Monogram* represented the larger world only selectively in its imagery. The manager was to find economic meaning in the factory's order; human relations were reserved for those initiated into the tribe.

General Electric Management Testifying to the Cause at Camp Commercial, c. 1925

Participants in Special Program at Camp Commercial, c. 1925

Interior View of Building 85, Schenectady, 1919

Phonograph Element and Motor Assembly Bench Conveyors, Building 26, Ft. Wayne, 1929

Meter Conveyor for Final Inspection of Watthour Meters, Building W, West Lynn, 1929

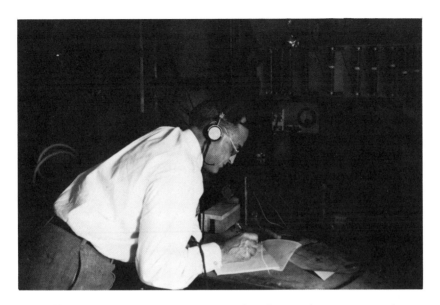

Dr. Willis R. Whitney in His Laboratory Listening to Electrons, c. 1910

Steinmetz at work at his retreat, n.d.

Steinmetz in His Laboratory, n.d.

Steinmetz on His Bicycle in Winter, c. 1895

Steinmetz on a Rock in the Mohawk River, n.d.

Tramway System, Barcelona, Spain, Typical Two Car Train in Station, c. 1930.

Sao Paulo Tramway and Light & Power Building in Sao Paulo, Brazil, 1929

Airplane View of Schenectady Works with New Bridge in Background, 1929

7

Consumers: The Corporation as History

There is no adequate history of advertising. Most of the works useful for understanding that history were written by participants in it and are therefore anecdotal and partial in their assessments. One of the best of these traces the history of a single agency.[1] Because of this deficiency much analysis of advertising photography has been almost entirely nonhistorical. Some of the most persuasive writing has been done by critics with a structuralist orientation, which leads them to dismiss historical dimensions of their object of study. Georges Péninou's *Intelligence de la publicité*, for example, devotes no space to the history of advertising but seeks to discover an intelligible language of visual discourse. Appropriately the work concludes with a series of visual examples showing how such devices as repetition, metaphor, synedoche, metonymy, first and third person discourse, and hyperbole are used in particular advertisements.[2] This approach has the advantage that it identifies devices in common use and might be likened to a rhetoric of late twentieth-century magazine advertising. Its disadvantage is that the place of that rhetoric in the larger culture cannot be assessed. When did it become technologically possible? And when was it actually in use? The other deficiency of the approach is that Péninou does not address the issue of competition in the marketplace—that is, why a company chooses a particular rhetorical device to sell its products.

Varda Langholz Leymore addresses this problem in *Hidden Myth*, whose subtitle, *Structure and Symbolism in Advertising*, accurately suggests the extensive use of Levi-Strauss's methods in her analysis. She examines not isolated advertisements but clusters of them, according to competing products. She shows the specific strategies employed in margarine and in butter commercials or the symbolism evoked by English and non-English cheese advertisements. The value of this approach is that one can understand particular instances as part of a larger pattern.[3] The problem remains, however, that one cannot discover from her analysis the more general constraints on mass advertisements, which can be made evident by examining their historical origin.

The kind of history needed is not one that recounts the formation of specific agencies or the precise dating of the first use of a technique but one that lays bare the social and economic conditions that first made magazine advertising desirable. Certain constraints inhibit the medium of magazine advertising, which inhere in its social function; one way to grasp this social function is to reconstruct the conditions that made such advertising necessary. In the case of the U.S. economy, it appears first in the period just after the Civil War, but a widespread or national kind of mass advertising did not emerge until the final decade of the century. When the electrical industry began in the 1870s, advertising still had a local character. Alfred Chandler noted that "in that decade only books, journals, and patent medicines were advertised on more than a regional basis. Nearly all other manufacturers left advertising to the wholesalers who marketed their goods."[4] The national market as such did not exist essentially because only in the 1880s were there enough monopolies or large corporations that could control a national distribution network. Before sales had a more personal basis in daily experience. A consumer knew the nearby city where a good was produced or had confidence in a particular store or wholesaler. It was possible to find out the reputation of a company or a particular store, and it was usually not possible to travel long distances to shop. Of course, some products were distributed nationally, particularly shoes from Lynn, Massachusetts, Colt revolvers from Hartford, Connecticut, and cotton and woolen cloth from New England mills. But it made no sense in 1860 to advertise nationally, and accordingly there were no forums for such advertisements.

The nationally distributed magazine advertisement was a unique historical product possible only at the end of the nineteenth century. In terms of a communication model the senders of such messages by then had emerged in sufficient numbers to make the mass market magazine possible. The new magazines of the 1890s, such as *Munsey's* and *McClure's*, were designed to appeal to the largest possible audience so that they could reach the emerging consumer market. The decision to use photography as the specific channel of communication was only one element in the construction of these new mass magazines. Had the halftone reproduction system not yet been perfected, engraving and woodblock printing could have served as a more than adequate channel. Indeed even though photography was available, engraving continued to play a large role until the 1930s. It will never be abandoned as an advertising tool because it permits the visualization of some ideas that photography does not.[5]

Nevertheless photography does possess attributes well suited to the requirements of a mass market. A photograph seems more veracious than a drawing; it appears to tell the consumer precisely what a product is like with a minimum of embellishment. It has a strong denotative function, while drawings appear to suggest or evoke. The photograph can depict a product inserted into a familiar context, showing it to be a natural part of the scene. A photograph offers vivid proof that a particular person—a celebrity or a social type—uses and endorses a product. And photographs compel a reader's attention far more than text and arguably more than drawings. Offering the illusion of the real, they are consumed at a glance. In the first forty years of their use photographs were almost entirely black and white; color images entered some magazines only in the 1930s. For the four decades before then black and white photographs contrasted with the color used in woodcuts and other hand-drawn forms, strengthening their claims to sober accuracy. The photograph thus emerged as an ideal channel of communication to the mass market for a variety of reasons. Although the use of photographs was a choice, not a necessity, they became more and more popular with advertisers because they possessed qualities unavailable in other forms of image reproduction.[6]

The nature of the mass market placed clear constraints on commercial photography. Advertising images necessarily appealed to a national audience. They sought to express not cultural differences but cultural regularities. They emphasized not regionalism but the nation, not class differences but democratic sameness, not diversity but social convergence. These characteristics inhered in mass market photography from the beginning, stemming from the terms of its historical emergence.

In its first quarter-century General Electric had little need of such national advertising. Selling electrical products primarily through salesmen and at trade fairs, it relied on human contact to market expensive heavy equipment. Direct contact with customers was essential to sell motors to cotton mills in South Carolina, small locomotives to Kentucky mining companies, or the entire system of electrical equipment used in the Panama Canal.[7] Large specialized orders shaped the company's marketing strategy in selling equipment to central generating stations, trolley cars, or sets of street lights to cities. Because of the nature of its business, the company did not address a mass market in its early years.

In contrast some corporations like the American Tobacco Company could exploit such a market as early as 1885. Because cigarette, flour, and canned goods manufacturers had all adopted continuous process machinery by the late 1880s, they could produce enormous quantities of goods.[8] Their sales were limited only by demand, which they could stimulate through extensive advertising. General Electric's process of production and its product line were far less standardized before 1900, and its customers' needs were far from uniform. Therefore it could not adopt a mass marketing sales strategy but continued to rely on salesmen in the field.

There was one exception to this generalization: the electric light bulb, a mass distribution item. Its advertising was not limited to direct salesmanship, nor was it left to the dealer's initiative. The earliest overt advertising photographs in the General Electric Archives deal almost exclusively with the electric light bulb.[9] The bulb was largely sold through wholesalers at first. By the 1880s large department stores had sprouted up in every major U.S. city, and by the turn of the century the chain store, such as those begun by F. W. Woolworth in 1879, had become widespread.[10] Through such outlets the new mass consumption reached the majority of the American public. Eventually light bulbs would be sold in drug stores, hardware stores, supermarkets, and many other retail outlets. Sales did not become a monopoly of a single franchise because market restriction did not advance electrification. Every light bulb display advertised the ubiquity of the electrical system. In addition restriction of bulb sales to a few retailers simply helped competitors.

Standardized and apparently interchangeable products created a new kind of marketing situation. Not only were the customers too numerous to address individually and sales now measured in millions of units, but more crucially, the difference between one company's products and those of its competitors could scarcely be identified. All light bulbs looked about the same. Light socket sizes were standardized. To sell one brand as opposed to another, advertising and trade name recognition became vital to success. What the bulb was and what it did were obvious; the virtue of any particular brand was not.

Ironically at the same time that electric lights were being greatly improved—between 1905 and 1915—General Electric found it necessary to adopt a sales strategy that emphasized not engineering advances but superior service. This strategy was adopted because innovations in light bulbs took place literally at a microscopic level, primarily in the filaments. While scientists made these more efficient and longer lasting, the overall appearance of a light bulb did not change significantly. The General Electric metallized (GEM) lamp, for example, was 25 percent more efficient than its predecessor, the improved Edison lamp. Yet both had a carbon filament, and they looked substantially the same. The significant difference was that the GEM filament had a tough graphite shell, which behaved like a metal at 1,900°F. The consumer could not see such things.[11]

If it was hard to distinguish between two brands of General Electric light bulbs, by the time the GEM lamp was marketed in 1905 many small companies could produce a reasonably good product that looked much the same. As with sales of cigarettes and other mass-produced items, advertising alone could create the consumer's perception of a difference. NELA and General Electric together inaugurated a vigorous advertising campaign in 1909. Significantly in that year they introduced no new light bulb, and the new brand name, Mazda, referred not to a particular kind of bulb but to the entire product line. The word itself had nothing to do with electrical technology; Mazda is the English name for the Persian god of light. It was hardly a word in common usage, and all of its associations had to be created through advertising.[12]

The magazines where these advertisements could be placed

fell into two main groups: older, literary magazines and brash new weeklies. The differences between these two measure the impact of mass market capitalism on American culture. The older periodicals were the inheritors of the gentleman's magazines and literary reviews of eighteenth-century England.[13] The *Atlantic Monthly, Harper's Magazine, Scribner's Magazine,* and *Outlook* served a genteel, educated class. Focusing on politics, religion, literature, and travel, their articles were often long, and they demanded a good deal of the reader. They carried virtually no advertising except for a few publisher's announcements, which were never allowed to break up the continuity of an article. These magazines employed a double-column format and usually printed all of an article together, so that a reader's concentration was not interrupted by the search for continuing pages in another part of the issue. The magazines were printed on good paper and usually contained wood-cuts. They were slow to adopt the halftone photographic process and included few illustrations in comparison to newspapers, which by 1910 had at least one per page.[14] The readership for such magazines was not large, ranging between 50,000 and 200,000. Their high price, twenty-five cents per monthly issue, discouraged many would-be buyers in an age when wages were roughly but two dollars per diem. With the exception of the *Nation,* none now survives in its original format, and even it has done so through the virtual elimination of illustrations and the use of cheaper, high-acid paper. The *Atlantic Monthly* and *Harper's Magazine* transformed themselves in the opposite direction, adopting the format characteristic of the new mass market magazines: extensive advertising, articles strung out through an issue, and a simplification of content to reach a larger audience. Disregarding these transformed survivors, the era of the literary monthly can be seen as the second half of the nineteenth century, with a gradual waning until the financial depression of the 1930s extinguished them.

Such magazines represented a national culture of a much different sort than that which the corporations required for the sale of their goods. Although it is tempting to consider the older literary magazines a form far superior to the new weeklies, they also had their drawbacks. They were possible because a cultural consensus existed in the middle and upper classes. The consensus was essentially Protestant and embraced the values of the older American stock. Feminists, radicals, blacks,

Indians, and the new Southern European immigrants did not have a voice in these periodicals. They reached an audience that listened approvingly to literary clergymen, gentlemen of letters, and university professors. At their best such magazines serially published the work of Henry James and Mark Twain and provided a forum for political and moral debate.

Significantly these magazines flourished in an era before academic specialization, when the professor still wrote for a larger audience of educated citizens. Before about 1880 academic disciplines did not have national conventions or separate publications; instead their work entered the public realm. It is mistaken to attribute the decline of these older magazines in influence and their eventual demise to the rise of mass market magazines. These appealed to another social class that did not read the literary magazines in the first place. Rather the class that had been the primary audience for the older, genteel magazine had begun to fragment by the early twentieth century. A host of new associations had begun to separate economists, historians, and political scientists from one another, to divide the humanities and the social sciences, beginning that devolution of intellectual life that has led by the 1980s to mutual incomprehension in the academic world and a separation between it and national culture.[15] At the same time the consensus of Protestant, white, middle-class values and the reification of those values in university curricula began to erode, undermining the ideological basis for the genteel magazine as well.

The corporation recognized these developments in practice. *General Electric Review* was an in-house example of the specialization of knowledge and professionalization of work that undercut the older reviews' readership. Similarly its *Works News* was an in-house version of a mass distribution magazine. Aimed at a lower social class, filled with short articles, it was lavishly illustrated compared to labor union magazines of the same period.

Works News followed the lead of magazines that had come into existence in the 1890s. These united the new photographic technology of the halftone process with the expanding mass market and became the principal channel of communication between corporations and consumers. The *American*, the *Saturday Evening Post*, and *Pictorial Review* each individually had a circulation twenty times that of the older literary magazines.[16]

They were packed with images yet cost only ten cents an issue because advertising defrayed much of the real cost. They reached the mass market four times a month and used more photographs because images sold magazines. These magazines, soon rivaled by imitators, received even more impetus from passage of federal legislation in 1905 that permitted companies to register and protect their trademarks. The older reviews benefited far less from this legislation, because of their high price and small audience, despite a belated decision to accept more advertising copy.

With this historical background the General Electric Mazda advertising campaign can be properly analyzed. It began by establishing a single slogan—"His Only Rival"—linked to a drawing. The advertisement serves as an excellent example of the advantages of drawing as opposed to photography in certain situations. The company wished to establish a connection between the power of the sun and the power of its light bulbs. This would be impossible to photograph but could easily be represented in a drawing of the earth in which the sun appears equal in size and power of illumination to a General Electric bulb. The unstated implication is that as the sun sets in the West, the electric light can effectively take its place. Below the drawing is the single line: "Get cheaper electric light from the Sun's only rival."[17]

Cheaper than what? Certainly not cheaper than sunlight. Such questions have nothing to do with national advertising. Their purpose is reiteration, linking a brand name with an image by repetition, not logic. The General Electric drawing appeared in the major magazines of 1910 and became synonymous with Mazda lamps. It appeared on all lamp cartons at least until 1916 and on most other promotional material as well. The drawing might appear fifty times in a single store window where stacks of Mazda bulbs were displayed, or it could be used as a decorative motif on printed materials.[18] One such use was on calendars General Electric gave away in 1913. In both store windows and on calendars, however, the drawing played a secondary role. Photographs became more important.

The calendars of 1913 came in two styles, identical except for the photograph. In one a bearded, older man in a turban holds a lighted bulb chest high. A photograph of this sort requires hours of careful planning and adjustments in the props and lighting to reach the desired effect.[19] The brilliant light high-lights his white beard, tunic, and turban, while his neck and shoulders cast dramatic shadows on the wall behind him. He appears to be a wise man, perhaps the Persian god Mazda himself, solemnly bearing the gift of light. His figure dominates the calendar cover.

In the photograph on the other calendar, the props were more lavish. A young woman stares impassively at the camera, holding a Mazda bulb high in each hand. Sitting on an elaborately carved wooden chair and wearing a sumptuous dress wound around her legs, its train fanned out on the floor, she is the image of Oriental splendor. The sunburst motif behind her head and the expensive Persian carpet under her feet suggest that she is of royal blood. The picture as a whole is symmetrical, from the pattern in the rug, to the chair, to her upraised hands, holding two bulbs equidistant from her face. She holds them as though they were religious objects, as does the magi on the other calendar. Together they suggest that the electric light is a timeless, spiritually uplifting object in essential harmony with the past. In these images the electric light is a miraculous gift, not a technological achievement.

This underlying theme recurred in other advertising pictures from the same period, using varying motifs. One gesture remained a constant: the light bulb itself was always held aloft in a human hand rather than screwed into a socket. Consider another magazine advertising photograph, that of a woman wearing a beaded and embroidered dress and diamond bracelets, who stares intently at a bulb while reclining on pillows. Even a snake that coils around her headdress arches as if to strike at the light she holds in her hand.[20] Such pictures tell the viewer nothing about the electric light as a technological device. Compared to the typical photographs of the *General Electric Review*, in which an electric light would be shot against a white background to show the bulb's filament, mass advertising images denote little. They are primarily connotative; the dress, the headdress, the painted silk pillows, and the billowing embroidered draperies together suggest the Orient, extravagant leisure, and upper-class luxury. The one thing these items cannot possibly connote is Western technology with its factories and machine shops.

The model's languorous pose emphasizes leisure so that the bulb partakes of her beauty and apparent availability. The photograph itself closely resembles an 1805 marble statue of Venus carved by Antonio Canova. Both figures recline at the same angle, with several pillows under the right arm. Each stares along the flat plane of the image rather than beyond its frame. But the statue's subject is the beauty of Venus, who symbolically holds an apple in her left hand, resting on her thigh, while the photograph shifts its emphasis from the woman to the electric light. It achieves this displacement in several ways: by clothing the model far more fully than Pauline Borghese, who modeled for the statue and is shown naked from the waist up; by lowering the right arm slightly, so that the eye is not drawn to the woman's face; and correspondingly by raising the left hand in the air, grasping the light bulb, so that it rests along the woman's line of sight. Venus offers us her profile as its own justification. The model's face turns more toward us, deemphasizing her profile while showing both eyes as they gaze at the bulb. The temptation of love has been replaced by the temptation to buy.

This was not the only borrowing from European art. A later photograph offers a virtual copy of Jacques Louis David's *Madame Récamier* (1800).[21] In each a woman in a white dress reclines on a chaise lounge, leaning on her left arm. In each a three-legged stand sits beside the divan at an identical distance from her curved back, as each face half turns toward the viewer. In both the right arm curves in a gentle arc along the body, the elbow just over the hip and the hand at the knee. Virtually the only difference in these two images is that the General Electric model holds a light bulb in her right hand. The copy has been so complete that it broachs on absurdity since the woman's dress and furniture are so clearly in the French Empire style.

General Electric's use of artistic models rather than technical information to sell light bulbs shows that it had learned what most advertisers understand: the consumer does not demand to know how something works or how it is produced as long as it can be appropriated. Ortega y Gasset noted that modern generations seem unconcerned with the social processes necessary to produce an automobile or an electric light, accepting each new machine as a natural development. Electric lights were in fact produced largely by young women much like those employed to advertise them.[22] Yet this fact was never used in advertising, for it would suggest that in order for some women to enjoy the electric light, others must be subjected to the drudgery of assembly line work. In that case the electric light would not be a pleasant new luxury item or a servant but the product of a perhaps oppressive industrial system.

It proved easier to efface the origins of the consumer product than to explain them. Advertisements did not discuss the technical basis of a device or the actual system used to produce it. If in the *General Electric Review* the corporation projected the image of an educational institution, in mass advertising it disregarded education entirely and inserted its products into inappropriate settings and landscapes. Not only was the Persian motif used for the electric light, but General Electric heavy machinery was displayed in a 1919 trade show with a Chinese theme.[23] Under a huge tent the electric companies erected pagodas and bamboo huts, strung paper lanterns that concealed powerful electric bulbs, and placed small potted trees, creating the semblance of an entire Chinese village. In the context of such a village with its overwhelmingly traditional associations, electrical machinery appeared to be a natural part of the preindustrial world. The show thereby effaced any distinction between premodern and industrial cultures. It conflated the imagery of an unchanging agricultural society with a radical new form of technology. In doing so the show more elaborately represented the same myth articulated by the symbol of the woman staring at an upraised electric light. Each brought together radically different elements and asserted their identity. A technology compatible with ancient Persia or traditional China was a nonthreatening technology. It did not transform society. It did not educate. It did not spring from a transformed industrial workplace. Rather it came fully formed into existence, blending with tradition.

An advertising float also photographed in 1919 made the same point but used different materials.[24] On it a group of women in long dresses sit casually on a green lawn. A trellis overgrown with roses helps create the sense of a pastoral setting, as do the shepherds' crooks that the women hold in their hands. The General Electric products at first are almost invisible in this pleasant Victorian landscape. They are nestled in the grass at the women's feet: electric coffee pots and toasters, as though sprouting from the garden. These consumer goods are immersed in preindustrial connotations. The float employs the same strategy of conflation used in the Mazda advertisements and the Chicago Electric Show. In each case the corporation has chosen to present its products not as a form of technology or as the outcome of a production process but as goods disconnected from history and merged with nature and unchanging tradition.

This method of advertising had its limitations, however, since it deemphasized novelty all together. By the early 1910s General Electric photographers began to depict landscapes of the new, such as the "Electric Heating and Cooking Devices in Mr. M. O. Troy's Residence, Schenectady, New York."[25] Today these electric coffee pots, hot plates, chafing dishes, and oven look quaint rather than modern. But to the viewer of 1912 they signified an entirely new kind of kitchen, without gas or coal, where for the first time heat could be applied to extremely localized areas and where electrical cords provided flexibility of organization. The row of black wall sockets at the back of the counter emphasized the modernity of this interior.

Such spaces appealed more to the consumer when they were in use, and General Electric distributed images of housewives sitting comfortably in easy chairs while an electric fan cooled them, or ironing comfortably by an open window, freed from the need to keep neat a hot stove, once used to reheat the iron. Such images provided appealing landscapes of change, interior spaces desirable not only for their novelty but for their comfort. To appeal in this way it proved unnecessary to reproduce an entire environment; a corner suggesting a certain style of living was sufficient. The apparent realism actually abstracted one or two elements and allowed them to stand for a larger whole in the viewer's imagination. The fetching young woman in her neat apron may be working, but she projects serene relaxation. She could be the maid in an upper-class home or a middle-class housewife. She may be the daughter or the young bride. Given the limitations of the setting, the viewer is free to make an appropriate connection suited to personal circumstances.

As advertising grew more sophisticated, the domestic market became more complex. Many small companies began to sell electrical appliances after World War I, forcing a change in General Electric marketing strategy. The efforts of in-house advertisers no longer appeared adequate, and the company turned to an advertising agency on a full-time basis for the first time. Bruce Barton's agency itself was the institutionalization of the changes in the marketplace that had occurred with the triumph of ogopolistic enterprises. In the mid-nineteenth century agencies had been responsible only for placing the advertisements, not for writing them. Gradually they began to assume more functions, suggesting methods, writing copy, and providing graphics and photographs. As their services increased, the agencies grew in size and number.[26] By the time General Electric went shopping for an agency, companies had begun to contract for a full range of services over a period of time.

The advantages of such contracts were many. Advertising could be planned as a long-term strategy. Whole campaigns could be coordinated so that not only particular products but the company name or a general concept could be sold at the same time. The piecemeal efforts of General Electric's dealers and in-house staff could now be replaced with a global vision of the market, with stratagems developed to reach many different groups with the most appropriate message. Thus to understand the individual advertisement it is essential to place it within the larger context of the campaign. Most previous studies have looked at only a random sampling of advertisements, without realizing that their placement was not random. One reason corporations relied on agencies was their ability to develop flexible techniques built on their knowledge of the marketplace. Under Barton's leadership, General Electric placed quite different advertisements in different periodicals.

Barton divided general magazines (as opposed to the small circulation trade magazines such as *Railway Age*) into eight groups. The division was based not on content or circulation figures but on a periodical's audience. Through judicious use of these groupings, suitable advertisements could be targeted so that in but one campaign they "were able to reach every farm home at least once a month, and every city home—large or small—twice a month."[27] Usually General Electric ran more than one campaign at a time. In 1924–1925 there were at least three: "Developing an Electrical Consciousness," which I will examine in detail here; "Make Your House a Home"; and "Any Woman Can." All three deployed a carefully constructed set of announcements in magazines selected from the master list, which was grouped into the following eight categories:[28]

Review periodicals (total circulation, 3,389,000):

Asia
Atlantic Monthly
Current History
Literary Digest
Magazine of Wall Street
McClure's
Mentor
Nation
National Geographic
Nation's Business

Nautilus
New Republic
Our World
Outlook
Review of Reviews
Survey Graphic
Time
Wide World
World's Work

General periodicals (total circulation 8,595,000):

American
American Legion Weekly
Century
Collier's
Cosmopolitan
Forbes
Harper's

Life
Red Book
Saturday Evening Post
Scribner's
Success
Sunset

Women's periodicals (total circulation 7,784,000):

Delineator
Holland's
Household

People's Home Journal
Pictorial Review
Woman's Home Companion

Country home periodicals (total circulation 607,000):

Better Homes and Gardens
Country Life
House Beautiful
Garden Magazine & Home Builder
Keith's Magazine for Home Builders

Juvenile periodicals (total circulation 710,000):

American Boy
Boy's Life
Youth's Companion

Scientific periodicals (total circulation 813,000):

Popular Mechanics
Popular Science Monthly
Science and Invention
Scientific American

Farm periodicals (total circulation 8,260,000):

Agricultural Engineering	*Progressive Farmer & Farm Women*
American Fruit Grower	*Southern Agriculturalist*
Capper's Farmer	*Successful Farming*
Country Gentleman	*California Cultivator*
Farm and Fireside	*Idaho Farmer*
Farm & Home	*Oregon Farmer*
Farm Journal	*Washington Farmer*
Farm Life	*Pacific Rural Press*
Farm Mechanics	*Power Farming*

Miscellaneous periodicals (total circulation 170,000):

American Federationist
Electrical Workers' Journal

A few magazines appear to be misplaced. *Literary Digest* would seem to be a general periodical, not a review; *Harper's* a review, not a general magazine. But on the whole the audience for each group of magazines makes sense. Review periodicals reach the educated class and include most of the older magazines. The general periodicals are those created since 1890, which reach the middle-class family. Women's magazines form a separate group because women were the consumers for only certain goods; refrigerators, for example, were the first product Barton chose to advertise based on surveys showing demand could be created for them.[29] Juvenile periodicals were far less important and usually carried educational advertising designed to give the corporation a good image. Country home magazines addressed suburbanites and the wealthier rural class, as opposed to farm periodicals. The large number of the latter is a reminder that in 1920 half of the nation's population still lived on farms and in small towns. Appropriately they were considered to be the second most important consumer group, after readers of general periodicals, and eighteen magazines were used. By comparison the company used only four scientific periodicals, none of them for specialists, an implicit admission that the advertisements' content was not technical. The smallest group of all is misleadingly labeled miscellaneous periodicals, when in fact they address workers. With a total circulation of only 170,000 compared to 8,259,650 subscribers in the farm audience, these labor journals reached but a tiny fraction of the working class. By 1925 General Electric itself employed half as many workers, and since it published house

Table 1
Number of advertisements on six subjects placed in
general circulation magazines, by audience, 1925

Audience	Trans-portation	Central Stations	Lighting	Indus-trial	Resi-dential	Rural	Total
Educated	15	17	18	25	18		93
Middle-class family	7	8	9	8	8		40
Women			3		12		15
Country gentry and suburbanites	6	1			7		14
Juvenile	4		1	5	1		11
Scientific	2	5	2	4			13
Labor	4	1	3	7	1		16
Farmer						55	55
Total	38	32	36	49	47	55	257

magazines to reach them, the near omission of workers is not an accident. The corporation had no interest in emphasizing class differences by supporting independent worker magazines. Its *Works News* encouraged employees to think of themselves as members of a community rather than as members of a social class. Beyond the factory the company's advertising represented a world of egalitarian consumption. Workers were to participate imaginatively in consumer choices and benefits. In that world they were members of families, not part of a working class.[30]

The corporation addressed these eight audiences through coordinated campaigns, each with its own theme. The theme itself was then broken down into specific subjects. For example, in 1925 General Electric used thirty-six separate advertisements between May and December with the general theme "Developing an Electrical Consciousness." It subdivided these thirty-six into six subject areas, which together covered the major product lines: transportation, central stations, lighting, industrial, residential, and rural. Table 1 maps the resulting marketing pattern.[31]

The table clearly demonstrates how completely farmers were separated from the rest of the consumption system. Raising the electrical consciousness of this group differed fundamentally from the same campaign in the cities and small towns. Farm advertisements had to do with production; all others concerned consumption. They were told nothing about central stations because the electric lines did not reach them in 1925. They read nothing about transportation because electric trolleys, subways, and tugboats were irrelevant to them. And for the same reason, none of the other audiences read about how to prolong the day artificially in hen houses during the winter and thus raise egg production or about how to milk more cows with a motorized milker. The urban and rural markets did not overlap. Periodicals such as *Farm Life* and *Farm Journal* had circulations over 1 million but reached almost exclusively one audience.[32]

The remaining two hundred advertisements were divided among the nonfarm audience unequally. The urban middle class already lived in homes wired for electricity. Developing their electrical consciousness in fact meant increasing their use of electricity. Thus the educated and middle-class audiences, including women and suburbanites, essentially were the General Electric urban market. The juvenile, scientific, and labor magazines combined received only forty advertisements (16 percent), and even this figure misrepresents their importance since the average circulation of these magazines was but 180,000. In contrast, the fifteen advertisements in women's magazines each reached an audience of 1.3 million, and the general periodicals were almost as large.[33]

Because General Electric's primary audience had already accepted lighting as a necessity, none of the advertisements under the category lighting concerned the home. Rather they advocated improved street lighting and more floodlighting of public buildings. These improvements allegedly would bring more business to town, reduce crime, improve safety, raise real estate values, decrease the number of traffic accidents, promote improvement, help the fire department, attract new industry, and better civic pride.[34] Central station advertisements emphasized that they were largely automated, safe, quiet, and clean facilities, which provided cheap electricity. The technical details of the unmanned power station were not explained. Rather the advertisements stressed the low cost of electricity compared to the cost of living. The thrust of the campaign therefore was to dispel any remaining doubts as to the usefulness and desirability of electrification in every area of life. Ideally the services would cease to be perceived as luxuries or novelties and pass into the realm of the natural. By 1925 this had already begun to occur with the electric light; it was not the subject of a single one of the thirty-six advertisements.

Unlike the prewar Mazda campaign, advertisements in the 1920s never suggested that electrification was miraculous or that the machines using electricity were unusual. Both had become inevitable parts of progress. The photographs made this point through pastoral imagery. The automatic power station stands in an isolated area on the Deerfield River surrounded by trees. The Los Angeles Railway substation is a beautifully design brick structure, standing back from the street surrounded by shrubs and a neatly mowed lawn.[35] Each station appears to blend into its surroundings, a noiseless and smokeless incursion into nature (Deerfield) and the city (Los Angeles) with minimal effects. These two photographs were used in more than twenty publications. They reiterated an image of tranquility, of harmony between the electrical industry and the American landscape.

Advertisements for the residential uses of electricity expressed another kind of harmony between technology and traditional values. These images comprised 80 percent of all the messages sent specifically to women, and they conform to what Ruth Cowen found characteristic in women's advertising in these years. The entrance of the new appliances into the market coincided with a rapid decrease in the number of servants in middle-class homes, which in turn transferred all the housework to the mother's new machines. Electrification decreased the physical labor in the home. Electric stoves were far cleaner than coal and wood stoves; electric washing machines eliminated a backbreaking chore; electric irons made ironing faster and cooler work in the summer. These and many other changes in household technology did not reduce the woman's labor, however; rather they transformed it. Cowen writes, "As the job of the housewife changed, the connected ideologies also changed: there was a clearly perceptible difference in the attitudes that women brought to housework before and after World War I."[36] At precisely the time when General Electric and other large corporations began to market consumer goods, work in the home was reconceived, particularly in advertising. Cowen summarizes these women's advertisements: "Before the war the trials of doing housework in a servantless house were discussed and they were regarded as just that—trials, necessary chores. . . . After the war, housework changed: it was no longer a trial and a chore, but something quite different—an emotional 'trip.' Laundering was not just laundering, but an expression of love. . . . Feeding the family was . . . a way to express the housewife's artistic inclinations."[37] A host of similar redefinitions in women's duties actually increased their average work week. Women were told to spend more time taking care of their children. They were encouraged to find emotional satisfaction in routinized tasks, which previously had been recognized as drudgery.

General Electric's residential advertising was part of the new ideology of housework. The most widely distributed piece of the campaign appeared in fifteen different magazines between April and July 1925, including all of the largest: *Saturday Evening Post, Literary Digest, Cosmopolitan, Pictorial Review, Household, Woman's Home Companion,* and the *American.*[38] Each of these reached more than 1 million subscribers. In total this single advertisement appeared 15 million times. Its form was determined by three historical circumstances. Given the mass market it appealed to, it necessarily had to emphasize cultural universals and regularities. Given the sophistication of the new advertising agencies, this appeal could be targeted at a specific segment of the mass market: women in the home. Given the transformation of home technologies implied in the new electrical appliances, the appeal would be to the emotional component of the newly defined role of homemaker.

The image satisfying these requirements proved to be one of a mother reading to her two children.[39] How can such a family group advertise electrification? Although the company monogram links the image and the corporate name, placing a seal of approval on motherhood does not in itself make it a company product. The text of the advertisement must be read to make a logical and emotional connection. It explains that because electricity supplies inexpensive power, mothers are free to do more important tasks: "This is the test of a successful mother—she puts first things first. She does not give to sweeping the time that belongs to her children." Mother does not own her time; the children govern her. Because of them, she must accede to the convenience of electrification. After all, as the copy continues, "An electric motor runs a vacuum cleaner for less than 2 cents an hour." This sentence appears in smaller typeface as a mere fact. But its position in the advertisement makes it part of an unstated argument, which runs: The cost of electrical technology is so small that its price is irrelevant when compared with the value of children. A mother has no real choice. To be successful she must acquire every available electrical convenience. "The wise woman delegates to electricity all that electricity can do." She must concentrate on the one task she cannot delegate to a machine: child rearing. "Human lives are in her keeping, their future is molded by her hands and heart. No lesser duties should interfere with the supreme duty of having plenty of time with the children." Mother seems independent, but the corporation dictates her role, ignoring all other possible kinds of parenthood that electrification might make possible. The company produces such an ideal mother as part of its ideology of consumption. By the logic of the advertisement, mothers who lived before electrification must have been failures.

The underlying logic of the text reinforces the first visual impression of the advertisement: General Electric produces modern motherhood and stamps a trademark on it. But this argument, implicit in layout and text, can never be stated directly since it is absurd. Rather the 15 million subscribers to magazines who saw this advertisement were to perceive that General Electric honored motherhood, that its products improved family life, and that electricity was an inexpensive servant. ". . . the letters G.E. are more than a trademark. They are an emblem of service."

Such statements cannot be found on the pages of the in-house publications, where captions remained descriptive. Indeed everything about the advertising image differs from the conventions of photography in the *Works News* or the *Monogram.* The advertisement incorporates many of the attributes of an illustrated lecture, welding together image and text much more tightly than in articles with photographs. In-house publications are entirely controlled and so do not need to merge text and photographs or design a small space that includes diagrams, several different typefaces, and a carefully shaped image. The *Works News* editors controlled the entire magazine and could make statements indirectly. They revisualized the plant while apparently only describing it, in photographs that had to appear to be windows on reality. But advertising by definition acknowledges that a message is being sent, and no intelligent viewer will accept the image component of an advertisement as a mirror of the world. Readers will not grant an objectivity to an advertising image because it transparently is an attempt to persuade. Consequently those who lay out advertising copy need not use photographs at all for their visual effects, and if they do use them, they need not preserve inviolate the rectangular space of the image. They are free to proclaim their use of codes openly as part of the transmission of the message.

Given this openness, an advertisement is far more successful when made part of a series, where certain images and ideas can be reiterated, thereby sending a second message in addition to the overt one. General Electric adopted this strategy in such advertisements as that on motherhood. It was but one of thirty-six advertisements, all of which contained three common elements: the name of the corporation, the monogram, and a small graph comparing the cost of electricity with the cost of living from 1914 to 1924. By repeating this graph and placing it near the corporate trademark, the company created an association between low costs and its products. Consider what is left out of such a graph. Are costs here calculated for home owners, for large users who always pay lower rates, or for a combination of the two? Is this cost the same for municipal and privately owned companies? How does this cost of electricity compare with the average family's electric bill, which presumably has grown much larger as more appliances are added? Such questions are never asked in these advertisements. Instead a simple juxtaposition, repeated in thirty-six different advertisements and displayed more than 100 million times, makes General Electric appear the guarantor of low electrical costs. The company expressed the purpose of this repetition only in the title for the campaign, "Developing an Electrical Consciousness," a title the public never saw. Thus an advertising campaign could omit the conclusion and purpose of its extended presentation.

After 1922 most company advertising had similar unstated secondary messages. It sought to make the General Electric logo a symbol of quality and service, and it attempted to alter public perception of electricity itself as much as it tried to sell any particular product. In the Mazda campaign, Persian mythology had been arbitrarily chosen to serve the corporation's needs. The Persian imagery had been overt and unambiguous. But in the 1920s General Electric wove its name into the fabric of American mythology. It adopted motherhood, efficiency, progress, and other watchwords of the culture, making the company appear to be the producer of these accepted values. General Electric thereby became an engine of history, an integral part of the culture, which could later claim, "Progress is our most important product." The corporation ceased to be a private interest; it became America.

Little in nineteenth-century American culture paralleled such advertising. Certainly in the sheer extent of its penetration, there was no precedent. Jacksonian Americans had developed a highly public form of politics, which used parades, barbecues, rallies, conventions, songs, and cartoons to reach voters. But these political forms were fundamentally democratic; corporate advertising was not. It is legitimate to assume that Jacksonian politics, revivalist religion, American landscape painting, and the literary renaissance of the 1850s defined a cultural moment and to treat these varied materials as independent parts that cohere. But it is not possible to survey the forms of mass culture in the twentieth century with the same assumptions. The corporation creates patterns of meaning wholesale and sells them to the public. It divides society into markets while ignoring fundamental divisions between workers and white-collar personnel, between regions, and between ethnic groups. The forms of mass culture, including world's fairs, magazines, advertising, corporate photography, commercial radio and television, and public relations, present a systematically controlled image of American society. These forms of communication and the large companies that control them must be linked in any investigation.

A focus on individual advertisements can lead only to erroneous conclusions. Not only is random sampling a foolish procedure when the distribution of advertisements has been carefully planned; not only is content analysis suspect when the theme of a whole campaign may never be stated except in corporate memoranda; not only can no personal expression of values be expected to be found; but a piecemeal approach to advertisements can lead to the conclusion that the attributes of the whole are those of the parts. Jackson Lears has summarized the thought of many recent critics who have made this error, including Jean Baudrillard, William Leiss, and Mark Poster.[40]

Confusion, diffusion, floating signs, collapsed references, banal images—the vocabulary differs but the emphases point to the same conclusion. All these authors would agree that the world created by advertisements gradually acquired an Alice-in-

Wonderland quality. It became a nether realm between truth and falsehood, where visual and verbal signs become detached from specific associations and meaning in general was eroded. There were only floating, detached images which (like the flickering faces in the movies) promised intense "real life" but kept it just out of reach. It was no wonder that, in the image empire of the consumer culture, day-to-day life began to seem curiously insubstantial, even unreal.[41]

The critics who make such arguments have concentrated on the individual messages of advertising and tried to imagine their reception. They have ignored the senders' purposes and assumed a diffuseness of corporate intentions congruent with the impression advertising creates. When an entire advertising campaign is examined as a unit, however, no such confusion, diffusion, or collapse of meaning is evident. Rather we see a calculated effort to obscure class differences, the promulgation of a national rather than a regional definition of American culture, a rejection of ethnicity in favor of homogeneous Americanization, a drive to increase electrical consumption, and a systematic redefinition of the role of women. Such goals are obscured in the individual advertisement. General Electric sent these messages more than 200 million times in the second half of 1925 alone.

The transformation of General Electric's advertising in the 1920s grew directly from the shift from in-house to external management. The efforts made before 1923 did not lack sophistication, drawing as they did on a wide variety of cultural resources, from French painting to Chinese architecture. But theirs was a sophistication concentrated within the photographic frame. Barton's agency specialized in understanding the audiences for images, subdividing the public into distinct groups. The in-house staff had deployed but a single strategy to reach everyone, as in the Mazda light campaign. The corporate use of advertising agencies, which generally began in the 1920s as it had at General Electric, marks an important structural change in society as a whole. The agencies did more than mediate between producers and consumers in the marketplace; they forged complex linkages connecting expectations, ideals, and certain products. And by heightening corporate awareness of its symbol-making role in society, advertising simultaneously prepared the way for equally large investments in public relations.

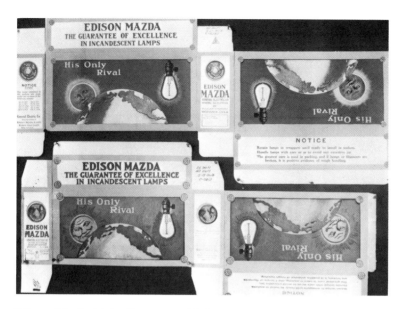

Edison Mazda Light Cartons, c. 1910

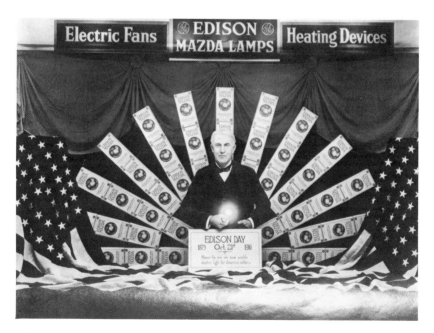

Edison Day Window Display, 1916

Incandescent Lamp Advertising Calendars No. 112 and 113 for Year 1913

Model on Couch, Holding G.E. Light Bulb

Madame Récamier, by Jacques Louis David, 1800. Reprinted courtesy of the Louvre Museum.

Chicago Electric Show, 1919

G.E. Float in Illinois Central Electrification Pageant Chicago, 1926

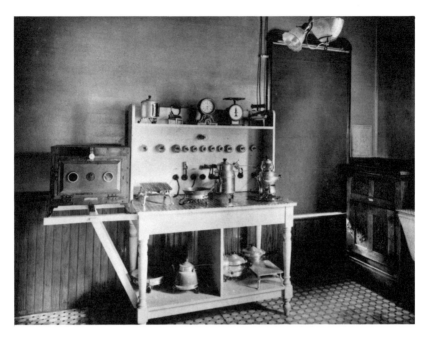

Electric Heating and Cooking Devices in Mr. M. O. Troy's Residence,
Schenectady, New York, c. 1912

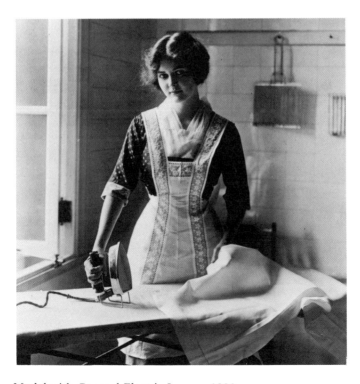

Model with General Electric Iron, c. 1920

MOTHER

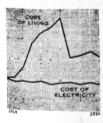

THIS is the test of a successful mother—she puts first things first. She does not give to sweeping the time that belongs to her children.

An electric motor runs a vacuum cleaner for less than 2 cents an hour.

She does not give to washing the time that belongs to her children.

An electric motor runs a washing machine for 3 cents an hour.

She does not rob the evening hours of their comfort because her home is dark.

To light a room splendidly, according to modern standards, costs less than 5 cents an hour.

Men are judged successful according to their power to delegate work. Similarly the wise woman delegates to electricity all that electricity can do.

She cannot delegate the one task most important. Human lives are in her keeping; their future is molded by her hands and heart. No lesser duties should interfere with the supreme duty of having plenty of time with the children.

Certainly no household drudgery should distract her, for this can be done by electricity at a cost of a few cents an hour.

GENERAL ELECTRIC

Reaching the Voter: The Invisible Corporation

One of the chief advantages of a public relations campaign over advertising is that of a potential multiplier effect. A good story will be reprinted, excerpted, and referred to by others, leading to additional free publicity. Edward Bernays, a leading public relations expert of the 1920s, recalled an impressive example of such a snowballing effect that occurred in 1929. Bernays gave an initial push to a campaign designed to celebrate the golden anniversary of the invention of the electric light by honoring Thomas Edison.[1] By the time his work was over, the entire United States had listened to Edison's dramatic re-creation of the electric light, narrated over one of the first international radio networks, and the U.S. government had issued a stamp in his honor. Bernays had so shaped and amplified the anniversary that it fundamentally differed from honors bestowed on previous heroes. Its meanings had been carefully prepared for months in advance; they only appeared to be the spontaneous expression of a culture.

In the twentieth century popular heroes and public debates have not always emerged from local perceptions. Increasingly they have been managed through public relations organizations eager to enhance their clients' positions. Nor have most public relations efforts been directed at so specific an event as Light's Golden Jubilee. More typically corporations have focused on general issues over long periods of time. During the four decades of General Electric's growth to dominance in the electrical industry, it was vitally concerned with the debate in American politics over who should own electric plants. The issue of public ownership became so common that it was a staple of high school and college debate. Handbooks explained both the affirmative and negative position to aspiring orators.

As early as 1906 the topic proved so popular that the Brooklyn Public Library prepared an annotated list of works on the subject, numbering more than seventy-five books.[2] Every newspaper carried editorials on public versus private utilities; every politician had to take a stand on the subject. Not a month went by when magazines such as the *Survey,* the *North American Review, Outlook,* and the *Review of Reviews* failed to carry an article on it. Each community debated the issue since it was a matter of local control, and in some cases they installed municipal plants. The majority of American electrification, however, remained private. While certain cities and many centers overseas chose municipal control, most American cities did not.[3]

The debate focused not only on lighting but on all other utilities as well. Advocates of municipal ownership called for elimination of private streetcar companies, gas works, lighting plants, telephone and telegraph companies, and in some cases railroads as well. Had they won the fight, U.S. city governments would have wielded much more power than they do today. More important, from General Electric's point of view, the nature of its market would have been quite different. The large electrical manufacturers made common cause with the private utilities, attacking public ownership on a wide front. Although many of their attacks were direct and above board, others were covert, utilizing third parties to discredit or to undermine opposing positions. These clandestine activities became the subject of a Senate-ordered investigation under the auspices of the Federal Trade Commission between 1928 and 1934.[4] Few have studied the findings of this investigation since the 1930s, however, and since the issue has cooled considerably in the interval, a brief summary of the two sides of the debate may be useful. In many respects the debate anticipated the present controversy over public versus private cable television systems and other similar issues.

Those for public ownership argued that utilities naturally devolved upon municipalities because they were uniform services that every citizen required.[5] Just as cities operated fire departments, water lines, and the highway system, used by all citizens, so too they ought to control the electrical power plant and the grid of lines that extended from it. Supporters argued that municipal ownership was not socialistic, in most cases attempting to separate the issue from overt ideology. They noted that the electrical system could not be regulated through competition and that it necessarily would be run as a monopoly. Private ownership of such a monopoly created many potential evils. Business could not operate efficiently without the check of competition, and private systems would therefore be wasteful. In addition to this waste the private system would be run for a profit. It would thus be tantamount to giving a private group the right to tax every citizen. A private utility might plunder the public, and it would not be held accountable. To protect its interests, such a monopoly necessarily would attempt to control local assemblymen and aldermen. Private utilities would therefore tend to bribe local officials; they would lower moral standards. And should they be run poorly, every citizen would pay for private mistakes, in effect violating the fundamental principle of no taxation without representation. Supporters of municipal ownership also pointed out that private owners would wish to expand consumption of electricity beyond necessary levels, installing more lighting systems in a town than were needed, for example. Such a monopoly would grow as much as possible, keeping its own interests ahead of those of the citizens.

Aside from these negative arguments, the supporters of municipal power saw clear advantages in public ownership.[6] It would remedy most of the evils of private monopoly by running plants for public benefit, lowering service rates, reducing taxes with any profits made, and avoiding needless investments. As a voter, every taxpayer would virtually be a stockholder in the public corporation, preventing corruption and mismanagement.

These arguments appealed strongly to the reform elements in American politics, particularly members of the short-lived Populist and Progressive parties. When properly presented, the municipal ownership position could appeal to most Americans on the same grounds that they preferred public to private police forces, water departments, libraries, fire companies, and the like.

But on the other side, proponents of laissez-faire economics and free enterprise made a powerful case for private control.[7] They attacked governmental expansion in any part of the private sector and argued that public corporations were generally mismanaged because they fell into the hands of corrupt politicians rather than being run on sound business principles and governed by self-interest. Public utilities would lose money because they did not need to make it. They would become a drain on the treasury, in effect raising taxes. The public clamor for low rates would weaken the financial position of the utilities, making investment in new equipment difficult, if not impossible. Furthermore public utilities would lose their most competent managers to private enterprises, which offered more room for advancement and remained alert to new technologies. Public managers would be underpaid and thus often incompetent. They would be subject to pressures with every shift in local politics. The utility itself would be forced to hire many political friends and relations. Instead of providing public service, it would provide jobs. Instead of lowering costs, it would increase them. Instead of making a community stronger, it would weaken an essential service while distracting politicians from their other tasks. After 1919 those against public utilities often advanced their position under the banner of anticommunism and antisocialism, adding a rather predictable rhetoric to their position. But even without that rhetoric they made a strong case, which could appeal to most Americans.

These positions had the appearance of logic, practical experience, and acceptable ideology. In the abstract either might be correct. Therefore most debates were lost or won based on actual case studies—communities where power cost more or less depending on whether it was public or private. As is usually the case in American politics, practical examples proved more important than theory, and most newspaper and magazine stories focused on a single incident or case to make a more general point.[8] Over a period of three decades before the Great Depression, Americans examined each municipality's system, seeking to find the general truth in the welter of facts. During much of the 1920s large projects such as the proposed damming of the Tennessee River Valley were hotly debated without resolving the issue of public versus private power.[9] The debate was not only defined by its intellectual content, however, but also through the means by which information reached the public.

Citizen groups were not the only adversaries in the debate. Large private utilities banded together to protect their economic interests, making NELA their umbrella organization after 1915. Thus NELA, which had previously served as a General Electric holding company, became a public relations organization, with a new headquarters in New York City.[10]

During World War I its activities were minor, but in the 1920s NELA ran an enormous public relations campaign against government ownership of utilities. This campaign addressed the entire American voting population, working through a wide variety of institutions, including the high schools, colleges, Rotary Clubs, women's clubs, newspapers, magazines, publishers, and virtually all other media and institutional forums. The scale and scope of this public relations effort was as large as the advertising campaigns of the same years, repeatedly reaching virtually every voting citizen.[11]

Most of these public relations efforts were covertly funded and did not bear any company name. For example, NELA supported a news agency in the Northwest that sent articles to newspapers in that region. Editors picked them up as news rather than as advertising and published them at no cost. Often the newspapers did not know the origin of the stories.[12] Across the nation NELA's publicity men distributed articles and even editorials that regularly appeared in the local papers. Some newspapers printed as much as 50 percent of all materials received.[13] The extent of the NELA's media penetration can best be understood through examples. During one year in Louisiana and Mississippi fifty-two newspapers carried more than 4,500 column inches of material. In New England during 1923 newspapers carried the equivalent of 156 pages and in Missouri, 334 pages of unacknowledged public relations. In both cases more than 10 percent appeared in the form of editorials and letters from prominent citizens. Many of these letters were in fact composed by the publicity committee and then signed by prominent local individuals.[14] Around the country the practices were similar; NELA had divided North America into regions and sent each the same materials. In short citizens received carefully prepared propaganda disguised as news on a regular basis.

NELA was only the initiator and coordinator of the campaign. Having lost its usefulness as a holding company in the economic realm, it became a publicity holding company, coordinating many apparently unrelated efforts throughout the electrical industry. Its sizable annual budget was miniscule compared to those of its many members, who often paid for local printing and distribution of materials. The Federal Trade Commission found that local utilities allotted 1.5 percent of their gross revenue for public relations and advertising, spending more than $25 million in 1927 alone. In many of these cases NELA provided literature and/or ideas, which the local organizations used. As a result estimates of the true cost of the NELA campaign cannot be made, but certainly overall expenses far exceeded its own budget.

Such covert communication has played an enormous role in American social and economic life in the twentieth century. It had disrupted the earlier processes that Americans had used to arrive at generally held opinions. A society that had cultivated debate and public oratory in the nineteenth century, in which many individuals had the opportunity to impress their views on local audiences, became a society dominated by a few centers of opinion, from which emanated a torrent of magazines, books, telegraphed opinions, and photographs. Through news bureaus and wire services organizations could unobtrusively insert material into public debate through third parties. The creation of NELA demonstrates that General Electric was not alone in understanding the benefits of such indirect communication. The organization included virtually every utility in North America, and other industrial sectors created similar institutions. These were collectively the logical extension of oligopolistic power, providing a favorable social context for the overt advertising messages of individual companies. Professional public relations firms developed almost entirely in the twentieth century as an ally of advertising, whose forms of influence proved far more versatile and influential almost as a direct function of their degree of indirectness.[15]

A small modification of Jakobson's model permits inclusion of covert communication and suggests how it differs from either advertising or in-house magazines. In the case of the *Works News* and the *Monogram*, the sender of the message was unambiguous, and its receiver knew what context to place the message within. But when a third party, such as a newspaper, acted as proxy for the real sender, the message's meaning changed for the receiver, who then encoded the messages as part of another context, accepting the false sender as the real one. There are interesting parallels to this situation in other apparently dissimilar communications. For example, in the circus, animals give performances, which a trainer directs and controls.[16] The animal responds to hidden cues but appears to be answering questions or obeying verbal commands. The audience watches the act without knowing how the trainer gets the animal to perform the tricks and does not see the covert cues and thus experiences the illusion of an animal with superior intelligence. Similarly, in the famous case of Clever Hans, a horse appeared to have extraordinary intelligence but in fact responded to cues that its owner himself was unaware that he gave to the animal.[17] The horse became celebrated for his apparent ability to add, subtract, multiply, and perform other complex operations, when in fact he only moved in accord with the tilt of his master's wide-brimmed hat. This unconscious communication was eventually discovered, and the horse was revealed to have no special powers.

In the case of Clever Hans or a circus act, communication only appears to occur between the audience and the animal. In actuality the audience communicates with the trainer, who uses the horse as an intermediary. Similarly in public relations, the newspaper only appears to address the public, serving as a conduit for a third party. Whether the editor has intentionally published public relations material or not does not change the structure at all from the audience's point of view. If the editor does not know where the material comes from, the structure is analogous to the communications of Clever Hans. If he does know, then the structure resembles the circus act, in which trainer and animal collaborate to create the illusion of intelligence where one expects none. Of course, at the circus, audience, trainer, and animal are present in one room. The audience knows that it has been tricked but has paid for that experience and expects it to be convincing. But in the case of corporate public relations, the three parties are widely separated in space and time. The communication does not occur in a privileged space where trickery and hidden cues are expected and permitted but in the arena of public debate. The public has not paid for the newspaper in order to receive covert advertising but rather to get accurate information.

But just as the public enjoys seeing a horse counting with its foot to reach the correct answer to a mathematical problem, while it would find the trainer's ability to solve the problem not only uninteresting but a poor performance indeed, so too the average citizen is far more impressed to find that a local banker, who apparently has no reason to favor private utility ownership, has taken time to write a thoughtful letter to the newspaper than to read a political advertisement. Just as the citizenry would boycott a circus where trainers replaced animals, so too it would not read a newspaper full of paid political announcements instead of news. The meaning of the message is enhanced if its origin is hidden. Public relations, in brief, consists of shifting contexts and changing speakers to deliver the message that advertising might also deliver but that few would bother to read, were its origin known.[18]

Although the message remains the same—indeed NELA often sent newspapers ready-made boilerplate that could be put right on the press—the context and the contact used to deliver that message have changed. As a result the receiver cannot code the message correctly, mistaking advertising for news. Even if NELA did not lie about content, it did falsify all the other constituents of the communication.

Furthermore there were cases when NELA distributed false information, making the deception total. For example, NELA spread incorrect statistics about the actual success of municipal power plants, creating the impression that they compared unfavorably with privately owned utilities. One conspicuous example of this practice was a handsomely printed pamphlet sent to every member of the U.S. Congress and to many universities in 1926.[19] E. A. Stewart of the Agricultural Engineering Department of the University of Minnesota authored the work, entitled "Electricity in Rural Districts Serviced by the Hydro-Electric Power Commission of the Province of Ontario, Canada." The booklet appeared under Stewart's name, with no reference to NELA, which had sponsored the research, paid for the printing, and mailed the result. Stewart was a well-known utility expert, and he filled his apparently scientific report with charts and statistics designed to prove that the largest public power project in North America—in Ontario Province—did not deliver electricity at a lower cost than private utilities. He concluded, "No miracle of cheap electricity is to be found on Ontario farms. . . . Nowhere in Ontario did I find actual cost of rural service out of line with the cost to the farmer in the United States." In fact, the case was quite the reverse; Ontario farmers paid on average only 40 percent of what American farmers paid for electricity.[20] This deception was not an isolated example but a matter of NELA policy. Time and again it distributed information purporting to show that municipal power companies had lost money or that they provided more expensive service than private companies in similar locations.

In these cases the entire communication became a falsehood, including not only the message but the apparent sender of that message, its social context, and the means of contact employed. Unlike the circus, where the chicanery is harmless, in the case of General Electric and its partner utilities in NELA, the trickery was worth millions of dollars in profits. Mastery of the media through public relations permitted the company to distort the political discussion on public ownership of the utilities. This appears to be an extreme statement of the case, but there are innumerable examples. Not only did NELA utilize bogus news agencies and cooperative college professors to disseminate its views, but it also encouraged the rewriting of school textbooks, published books for school libraries, campaigned for removal of other books from the curriculum, sponsored conferences, endowed scholarship funds, supported university research favorable to its interests, paid speakers to travel around the country expounding correct views, sponsored essay contests, made noninterest-bearing deposits in banks to secure their support, broadcast to more than 10 million persons a year over the radio, and sought to spread NELA opinions through civic and professional organizations in the insurance industry and through members' contacts with chambers of commerce.[21] The total effect of these activities cannot easily be assessed or summarized since they lasted more than a decade and cost more than $10 million in direct expenses to NELA, as well as many other costs borne by the individual utilities that were members.

These activities came to light only because the U.S. Senate launched an investigation into the utility corporations, carried out by the Federal Trade Commission between 1928 and 1934. The results of that inquiry filled more than 11,000 pages. General Electric's involvement was extensive but well hidden. The corporation's name scarcely appears in the 500-page index, and the origin of NELA as a General Electric holding company escaped the investigators' attention. Nor did the Federal Trade Commission emphasize the extensive involvement of General Electric's chief officers in the NELA campaign, except in brief notes. Owen D. Young, chairman of the board, served on the powerful publication committee. Gerard Swope, company president, helped to distribute 33,000 copies of a NELA pamphlet entitled, "A Symposium: Common Interdependence of Labor and Electric Power in the United States."[22] And Bruce

Barton, the company's chief advertising adviser, served NELA in a similar capacity. He authored an article for the first issue of its magazine, *Light*, and throughout the 1920s prepared envelope enclosures that utility companies inserted with their monthly bills. They were called, inside NELA, "Bruce Barton envelope stuffers." He regularly received a retainer of $5,000 for his services, which included the preparation of short booklets. In 1926 NELA spent $199,000 just to print them.[23]

As these examples demonstrate, General Electric's chief officers and advertising adviser were intimately involved in the publicity efforts. NELA's total budget for these activities rose from just over $500,000 in 1923, to more than $1 million in 1928. General Electric contributed something more as well in the form of services from its Publicity Department, with its staff of over 200 professional artists, photographers, and writers. In particular it lent NELA one of its most effective public speakers, Charles M. Ripley, who had previously written two classic works of welfare capitalism, *Life in a Large Manufacturing Plant* and *The Romance of a Great Factory*. In the last years of the 1920s Ripley traveled widely, delivering an illustrated lecture entitled "The Romance of Power."[24] In four months alone, beginning in September 1927, he gave the lecture more than one hundred times at an expense to NELA of $3,100. During the first three weeks of this tour, Ripley reached twenty audiences in Ohio, Indiana, Kentucky, and West Virginia. His travel had been carefully planned to minimize backtracking or wasted motion, and he often delivered his lecture more than once a day. He regaled the Youngstown Optimist Club, the Warren Ohio Kiwanis Club, the Cleveland Engineering Society, the Akron Rotary Club, and many schools as well. In those three weeks he spoke to 6,500 business and community leaders, answering their questions and arguing for the private ownership of power. Ripley's talk proved so successful that NELA decided to print 27,000 copies, which it then distributed to schools and colleges.[25]

Although he was active in this work for several years, Ripley could not travel widely enough to suit his superiors. NELA therefore made 50 copies of the 104 slides that formed the visual core of his talk and sent out trained lecturers to every part of the country to deliver it.[26] The extensive use of slides in the lecture highlights another difference between covert and overt public relations. While General Electric used images extensively in its in-house publications, NELA used fewer. In the case of the covert newspaper message, photographs were not needed in order to make the communication appear to be objective. The reasons for this difference were hardly economic, since both organizations had immense sums of money to spend. Rather the corporation needed the photograph as an apparently unbiased form of evidence whenever it communicated directly with its employees or the public. The photograph seemed a neutral and unbiased element supporting the company message. Not only were photographs unnecessary in the newspaper, which itself was the guarantor of objectivity, but photographs could even raise questions of credibility. The reader seldom asks the origin of a news story even if it arrives from a distant location to the local newspaper. Unusual photographs, however, particularly if taken inside factory gates, could arouse the suspicion of bias that the use of the newspaper was to allay.[27]

Perhaps a more pragmatic reason also influenced NELA's decision not to use photographs extensively. Its materials generally were prepared in New York in such a way that they later could be adapted to local conditions. A typical story would be rewritten by the local bureau, adding the names of pertinent local companies and cities, as well as the names of local citizens. Photographs were not sufficiently general to be adapted to the many localities where NELA's publicity appeared. The very concreteness of photographs, which ensured and compelled belief, also limited their use.[28]

In the case of the Ripley "Romance of Power" lecture, however, personal bias could not be hidden, and the photograph reappeared as a strategic ally of corporate truth. In the darkened hall, Ripley or his fifty surrogates remained invisible while the audience displaced its attention to the slides. Thus the apparent exception to the general rule that NELA preferred not to use many photographs proves its accuracy. The slides performed the objectifying function otherwise performed by the newspaper. They authenticated the speaker's argument in situations where the audience could see him and know the origin of the message. In effect the photographs played the same role as the trained animal in the circus, apparently acting as independent agents in tandem with the speaker's remarks. Of course the circus animal lives, and the photographs only echo moments of life, but the structural parallel remains the same. In each case communication takes place through a slight of hand. Just as the trainer has prepared the animal over many months to respond to hidden cues, so too corporate photographs seem to depict the world but only mirror the corporation's view of it.

Once an audience accepts the substitution of an image for reality, the accompanying text stands in a new relation to it. The photograph becomes the signified, or the point of reference, while the text becomes its signifier. And since the reader has access to both, he or she will naturally prefer to look at the real thing rather than read about it. The text only seems to explain the photograph, when in fact the image legitimizes the text's description of it. The words spoken by a traveling lecturer to an illustrated talk stand in the same relation to a photograph as do the words of an article whose origin is known. In each case the photograph acts as a decentering device, pulling attention away from an argument that the corporation wishes to make and permitting it to pass as commentary. Only in public relations can such a powerful tool be discarded since a newspaper provides another kind of blind for the corporation to hide behind. Photography might seem to be an ideal or even indispensable tool in public relations, but in practice it has less need of photographs than either advertising or in-house magazines. This is because both it and corporate photography are ideological forms that masquerade as objective truth. Combining them in one communication is not only redundant, it may inadvertently reveal to an audience the difference between the overt and the covert senders of the message.

Overall NELA's public relations activities reveal, first, the limits of photography as a means of communication, and second, the differences between in-house publications and public forums of communication. The magazines addressed to engineers, workers, and managers contained many company photographs, often virtually without comment in the articles they accompanied. Such images were not presented as evidence to prove an argument but as transcriptions of reality. In advertising and public relations the photograph necessarily becomes more problematic, although its status is not the same in each of these. The advertising image is unequivocally presented as part of an argument in favor of a product, and having lost its status as pure transcription of the world, the text itself can invade the frame. Words are routinely superimposed on the sky or the ground of these photographs, which in any case make no claim to be objective truth. In contrast public relations must aspire to the appearance of objectivity, yet to do so it must also hide its origin by placing third parties between the sender and the receiver of its messages. Public relations can use photographs, therefore, only if the third party plausibly could have had them. Otherwise the sender's identity becomes an issue, undermining the audience's confidence in the message. Photographs, though not by nature true, prove to be less versatile than language when it comes to falsehood. They are irretrievably linked to the site they depict, while writing is not so attached to the place where it was done. Photographs are ideological, not mechanically objective, but theirs is an ideology of identifiable physical relations, both within the frame and between the cameraman and the site. General Electric could easily use photographs to construct image worlds for its own employees through a selective presentation of itself. With equal ease it could depict landscapes of desire for consumers. But NELA could not easily make photographs for third parties engaged in public debate. And when introduced, they served not to constitute a social world but rather to illustrate an argument.

9

Conclusion: Photography as Ideology

Industrial photographic archives make possible a new kind of corporate and social history. In it, photographs will not illustrate arguments; they will be understood as visualizations of ideology. Wherever a company photographer pointed his lens lay a subject that the corporation wished to interpret, and it is these interpretations that need to be studied. Business history is more than the story of balance sheets, labor relations, successes and defeats in the marketplace, and inventions. To survive, a corporation must provide employees and customers with interpretations of the world. It must project not merely a good public image but a construction of reality that organizes the dispersed facts of experience. This construction of social worlds was necessary for the functioning of large corporations, and photography proved to be an ideal medium of corporate self-representation.

This book has examined one exemplary archive as a visualization of corporate ideology. By studying the production, dissemination, and historical setting of General Electric's photographs, it has identified four sets of self-representations that developed and coexisted between about 1900 and 1930. Its organization emphasizes the corporation as a communicator, the medium of photography, and the audiences addressed. In principle there is no reason why such an investigation could not also be directed at a company's commercial art, its films, or other forms of expression. But photography, apparently realistic and easily disseminated through magazines and newspapers during the time period, was the dominant practice.

Few companies would be better suited to such an investigation than General Electric. It early dominated the electrical markets and then maintained a position as one of the ten largest U.S. corporations. It sold a wide range of products, from turbines and generators to electric light bulbs, from heavy industrial machines to domestic appliances. And its organization was representative. As Chandler noted in his history of management in U.S. business, "The structure built at General Electric became and remains today a standard way of organizing a modern integrated industrial enterprise."[1] The photographic department was a necessary part of this organization, taking much the same form in other corporations, such as General Motors, International Harvester, and the United States Rubber Company. Each required large numbers of images to improve internal communication and advertising. Like General Electric they had to reach and persuade quite different audiences in order to maintain a strong market position, coordinate the vertical integration of their various enterprises, and deal with their work forces. These similar structures and needs, not surprisingly, led to comparable image requirements.

Judging by the photographs that appeared in other company magazines and the few articles written about corporate photographic staffs, General Electric's archive of images, like the company, is representative. Its photographs were unsigned and produced by a group. They clearly fell into clusters of related images, treating recurrent subjects with standardized techniques. Its photographers kept abreast of changes in their profession through membership in associations and by reading specialized magazines. They worked within technological limitations imposed both by the photographic equipment of their day and by the reproductive capacities of the halftone printing process. However, conventions developed within commercial photography, rather than these limitations, proved central in the development of a unifying aesthetic. While the major codes of corporate self-representation can easily be detected, an image's meaning and purpose cannot be discovered in the archive. It cannot be understood apart from its context and audience. General Electric, like most corporations, used a range of both in-house and national magazines, each targeted for a certain group.

This proliferation of images and contexts cannot be regarded as part of a conspiracy or self-conscious program of domination. The evidence at General Electric points to a gradual development of image classes as the need arose for specific magazines. Varying photographs were called into being by changing social and economic conditions. No one articulated a theory of industrial photography. Rather these images were secondary effects, products of the marketplace. The *General Electric Review* began as a service to salesmen and then became a vehicle to reach engineers directly with technical information concerning new products. The *Works News* began in 1917 as an outgrowth of a program of welfare capitalism, and the *Monogram* emerged in the early 1920s to address middle management. In these cases and most obviously in advertising itself, the demand for photographs came as the result of outside conditions.

The different origins of the demand for photographs should not obscure the underlying linkages between these demands and the industrial system. The nature of electrification determined a profitable sequence of technical development, such that electrical lighting served as an entering wedge in the market, followed by heavy industrial equipment and only then allowing for the development of consumer goods. This sequence in turn determined the emergence of new audiences that General Electric would address. The only early advertising in popular magazines was for electric lighting itself. As the electrical grid spread, electrification of industry became easier, and by 1903 General Electric needed to reach an audience of engineering specialists. Sales of heavy industrial equipment in turn created a demand for larger generating capacity and spurred further expansion of the distribution system. These successes led to growth and differentiation of the labor force as blue-collar work became subdivided and repetitive, while the numbers of middle managers increased. Both changes created new internal audiences. Thus an interlinking system of technical, economic, and managerial imperatives underlay the sequence of audience emergence.

As audiences increased so did the volume of images produced in the photographic department. By the 1920s it made more than 1 million prints a year from new negatives and from a backfile of 300,000 that grew by more than 10,000 accessions each year. To work at this pace, the staff subdivided the work and mechanized it as much as possible so that no individual created any photograph from start to finish. Under these circumstances, although the images did visualize corporate ideas and attitudes, this result did not arise from individual initiative or from censorship. Rather the treatment of subjects became standardized, with recognizable conventions. Each class of images had its rules of construction. In portraiture, for example, managers and engineers were taken at an intimate distance against a neutral background, in imitation of practices first developed in painting. In contrast inventors appeared in a recognizable context, at work, usually holding a new apparatus. Employing such image classes, the industrial photographer could work rapidly and effectively without the need to invent a new point of view and procedure for each subject.

Industrial photography should not, therefore, be considered a single genre. It consisted of a set of representational strategies that varied from one subject to the next and that often originated elsewhere. For example, the *Review* adopted conventions from mechanical drawing to depict isolated machines; the *Monogram* used the informality of the snapshot to show executives on retreat at Association Island; and the *Works News* borrowed the group portraiture common in high school yearbooks to depict worker sports teams. The largely derivative nature of industrial photography, however, should not suggest that it simply repeated previous forms. Commercial cameramen reworked older conventions, and their photographs acquired new meanings when inserted in corporate publications and national magazines.

Industrial photography did not achieve coherence as a single genre but harmonized its many forms of representation through the use of a common aesthetic. In part the subdivision of photographic labor and the mechanization of developing and printing imposed this aesthetic. For example, cameramen learned to avoid strong contrasts of light and shadow when possible because it was difficult to print from these negatives. They also tried to avoid carrying a wide variety of photographic plates, not only because they were heavy but also because different plates required separate handling in the darkroom. An industrial aesthetic supplemented such technical constraints. Eschewing the soft focus and stylized treatment of space commonly used by pictorialists or the search for symmetry, balance, and dramatic contrasts common to many other artistic photographers, commercial cameramen did not call attention to their craft. They made industrial landscapes and products familiar and comprehensible, often through the use of unusual devices and techniques. However they were achieved, industrial photographs appeared to be transparent windows revealing a natural subject that had not been tampered with.

Together the repertoire of representational strategies, harmonized by an underlying aesthetic, resembles a rhetorical system. This system served a social function, shaping the communication between General Electric and its audiences. Indeed these photographs were never presented alone as works of art but rather appeared in conjunction with written texts. The relationship between word and image was not merely that of illustration. The photographs concretized ideas that often remained unstated in the accompanying text, as in the images of individualistic labor on the covers of the *Works News* or the quite different treatment of workers as units of measurement seen by engineers who read the *Review*. Such photographs completed messages implicit in the text and the context where they appeared. Photographs performed this task while seeming to be nothing more than ordinary statements. Apparently mere descriptions, they served as forms of argument, making debatable statements about the position of workers, the role of managers, the nature of industrial products, the effect of consumer goods on the family, and the impact of electrification on society. Despite their immediate appearance as commonplace glimpses, indeed as rather artless constructions, such photographs conveyed corporate ideology. They did so not haphazardly but systematically, in image classes appropriate for each audience.

Because this marshaling of images into a system of representation took place without an articulated theory, it raises a question about intentionality. What gives the quality of logic to this image production? The facile answer would be that photography served as an instrument of class domination used by management to create and sustain its hegemony. But this proves to be an oversimplified explanation. The evidence suggests that no one consciously intended to use photography as ideology. The routinized labor of the photographers, the way in which each magazine or image market emerged in response to outside necessity, and most important, the many contradictions between the image classes themselves suggest that the creation of these classes was an unintended outcome of the functioning of the corporation as a whole. These images did not embody a unified system of beliefs that one group imposed on another but rather were a discontinuous system—a series of mutually contradictory statements made to a number of groups. These photographic forms served as an effective vehicle for communication, in short, but analysis reveals no overarching ideology, no conscious attempt at class domination, and no awareness that any code was being employed.

Nor should this situation appear unusual to anyone knowledgeable in the fields of semiotics or linguistics. Native speakers who use their language flawlessly often can give no account of its grammar. Many other codes of communication are employed unself-consciously, as in the gestures that every human being uses to amplify and enrich speech. Corporate photography is but one more instance of a system of meanings that developed without first having a self-conscious grammar, rhetoric, or program. As in speech and gesture, corporate photography developed a coded system of communication without its creators being aware that they had constructed it. A final proof of their lack of awareness is the disorganization of the resulting photographic archive, built up from 1892 until the early 1960s. Despite extensive cataloging efforts the archive eventually fell into neglect because few in the corporation could understand it. The finding aids to the whole collection rested on a subject-oriented classification system, while the filing system proceeded chronologically. It was like a library where books had been cataloged only by title, with the volumes arranged on the shelves in the order that they had been purchased. As the collection grew to more than 1 million images, it became a maze of misplaced or mislabeled photographs, lost filing cards, and inevitably important photographs that the staff had refiled where they could be easily found. No one in the corporation understood these images as a coded system of communication or as a form of ideology. They were simply a rather scrambled file of old photographs.

The quality of logic that one can find in the image system developed not from any intentions but from an interlocking set of constraints that was common to most large corporations in the years from 1890 until 1930. As a group they moved from producing heavy industrial machinery toward more consumer goods, from artisanal work forces to industrial blue-collar workers in increasingly routinized factories, from direct ownership of factories toward a managerial system. During this period of change most corporations created their own photographic staffs, who found it necessary to routinize production.

Standardized image classes resulted from the confluence of common subject material, the same photographic and reproductive technology, and the need to address audiences of workers, technicians, managers, and consumers. The photographs expressed the divisions between these audiences in both their choice of subjects and the treatment of them. Corporate photography was shaped by the larger constraints of its historical position. Far from being a simple matter of conscious choice, it was a coded system constituted by economic, technical, and social pressures.

At the same time, however, the photographic images themselves had a reciprocal effect on social systems. For example, an image of individualistic work displayed on the cover of a magazine for blue-collar workers plays a role in the ideological formation of those workers even if they consciously resist company public relations. Similarly an engineer who regularly reads a technical review where other engineers are consistently depicted as part of management receives a set of messages about how to conceive of the self, other workers, the company, and the impact of technology. Such images instigate social norms. They do not simply reify or reflect existing conditions. Rather these image classes themselves help to constitute the social worlds that they then address. The photographs produced at General Electric imposed the appearance of logic and naturalness on newly created programs that extended corporate power. They legitimated the new research and development arm of the company, presenting the corporation as an educational and scientific institution. While offering this vision of itself to engineers, the company developed another set of images to legitimate welfare capitalism to its workers, reinterpreting the factory experience so that it consisted of individualist work, sports, educational programs, and a variety of benefits welding the corporation into a community. For middle management yet another group of images represented the company in terms of profits, the control of vast spaces, international markets, and personal success founded on cooperation. For consumers the company offered yet another vision of itself as a guarantor of social values, better living conditions, and progress. By exemplifying varying forms of social status and by offering visualizations of desirable products, the company's photographs offered a compelling construction of reality for each audience.

Thus, if these images emerged from the necessities of corporate communication and from routinized work in the photographic department, they nevertheless did not serve to reinforce or reify an older social order but to visualize a new one. They reiterated not a single ideology but rather a group of ideologies, each suited to its audience and therefore instrumentally linked to the corporation's necessities, even if their philosophies were inconsistent with each other. General Electric could not be at once an educational and scientific institution, a welfare institution, an organization bent on profits, and a public servitor. But it could and did present itself as each of these things to separate audiences. No one saw inconsistencies in the corporation's presentations of itself because the audiences did not overlap. The individual photographs each seemed to be objective statements of facts such as the audience knew them. They concretized otherwise unspoken assumptions about the social order and helped establish work hierarchies, social roles, and group attitudes.

These photographs did not serve as mirrors of reality or as pictures of an older social reality that was slipping away. Rather they provided corporate stability at moments of transition. For the engineers and technicians the change came just after the turn of the century. An older set of social roles, in which inventors and engineers were simultaneously workers, managers, investigators, and manufacturers, had begun to break down. The professionalization of engineering required a narrowing of these options and an identification of technology with science. The images employed in the *General Electric Review* fulfilled these requirements. They referred not to workers or the processes of production but to abstract ideas, finished machines, and engineers dressed as managers. Blue-collar workers faced another transition: from craft labor to large factories, subdivided by function, using assembly lines. The photographs in *Works News* offered them a reconception of their role in the factory, removing them from the workplace as a group and inserting them in other contexts while preserving an ideology of individualistic labor. Managers faced quite a different transition, from direct contact with and control over the company to a system of subdivided responsibilities that required professionalism. Coming from many backgrounds, they required a new definition of their position and social role, and they found both in the *Monogram* and the camps at Association Island. In all these cases photography served not to objectify already existing social relations but to visualize new ones. It assisted the development of a pluralistic corporate ideology in which General Electric legitimized varying interpretations of itself.

Nor was this all. Corporations influenced the realm of photography as a whole. They employed thousands of professionals who influenced photographic magazines and national meetings. These photographers assimilated the representational strategies of art and documentary photography when they proved useful. Most important, their own images reappeared billions of times. General Electric's advertising, but one part of its photographic effort, reached every American family twice a month during the 1920s. Multiply this figure by the number of large corporations, double the result to include nonadvertising efforts, and then compare this total with attendance at photographic exhibitions in the same years. The corporate sponsors of photography had established by about 1925 an economy of image production. Not only did they employ large numbers of photographers; not only did they exhibit thousands of images to each citizen every year; but they also established a common aesthetic. Photography had become a central social practice in the maintenance of mass culture and an important precursor to television, itself developed in part at General Electric.[2]

Fine art photography can be understood only in its complex relations to this dominant image economy. Significantly Alfred Stieglitz began to champion photography as a fine art, with some success, at the time when corporate photography emerged. When the halftone made the mass production of images possible in newspapers and magazines, Stieglitz began to publish a fine art journal based on photogravure, a more exacting form of reproduction that enabled him to sell high-quality limited editions.[3] These two forms of image marketing catered to quite different audiences, reproducing the split between elitist art and commerce. The distinction was not merely one of education but rather a difference in aesthetics that went deeper than a contrast of styles, as for example that which commercial realism opposed to pictorialism. Fine art photography itself had many divergent styles, including what Frederick H. Evans advocated as pure photography in opposition to pictorialism.[4] The distinction between commercial and fine art work lay in a much different question. Stieglitz was typical in his praise of originality in photography, not only in the sense of original design but in the more commercial sense of the first or the only. By destroying negatives or refusing to make more prints, a photographer established an image's uniqueness.

In contrast the commercial photographer's work was intended to be reproduced, and the social roles, products, and electrified landscapes he depicted were to be understood as being reproducible. The social function of corporate photography harmonized with its aesthetic. In Walter Benjamin's terms the prestige of art rests on its aura of originality, which, however, diminishes as more and better copies become available.[5] In the twentieth century because of reproduction, no work of art remains a unique experience, available at only one site. From this perspective Stieglitz's efforts to preserve photography's originality were but a holding action against the general movement toward the mechanical reproduction of art. Corporate photography exemplifies this movement in its extreme form through an aesthetic that hides its artful creation in order to promote reproduction itself as a social value.

This contrast between the values of artistic and commercial work should not obscure the ease with which a particular style could move from one to the other. Given the artificiality of realism itself, the perception of what the world was like could easily undergo transformations. We have already seen how General Electric deployed varying photographic styles for each of its audiences without abandoning a realistic presentation for any of them. But perhaps the most striking form of realism came in the later 1920s when industrial landscape photography became an important and lucrative new genre. The early work by occasional pictorialists who tried industrial subjects, such as Alvin Langdon Coburn, had characteristically turned steam and smoke into atmospheric effects that complemented an impressionistic style. But in the 1920s a new kind of image appeared far more appropriate to the emerging managerial class. Now often called precisionism because of its relation to a movement in painting of that name but then also known as straight photography, the new style was developed by Edward and Brett Weston, Charles Sheeler, Margaret Bourke-White, Sonya Noskowiak, and Imogen Cunningham.[6] Their images further emphasized the tendency toward abstraction already visible in earlier in-house publications. Many corporations began to employ these artists on a freelance basis. Their work, as in Sheeler's images of the Ford River Rouge Plant from 1927, depicts a hard-edged, rhythmic world of man-made forms, devoid of grass, trees, and other natural elements. The factories are vast yet orderly, massive yet sculpted in clean lines. By the early 1930s, this industrial sublime became a staple of corporate production, lifting industry to a heroic scale, depicting factories as uncluttered, monumental forms thrust into the sky or carved into the earth.[7] The style quickly found a national audience in *Fortune Magazine*, which began publication in 1929.

Nor was this the only example of business's capacity to stimulate and/or absorb other styles. In worker-oriented magazines it had successfully assimilated the documentary, including the work of Lewis Hine himself. By the 1940s it proved equally possible to incorporate 1930s documentary within a corporate structure. Standard Oil hired Roy Stryker, former director of the Farm Security Administration photographic project, to run a documentary bureau that would depict in the most general terms anything related to their operations. The resulting photographs retained much of the style of 1930s documentary work but were adapted to in-house magazines for managers, where most of them appeared.[8] Thus corporate photography did not remain static but assimilated other representational strategies. As the dominant practice in the economy of image production, corporate work resituates other photographic practices that until now have been studied in isolation from it. The history of photography becomes the study of a network of interrelations and oppositions between these practices rather than a survey of new technologies and master artists. A full history would not isolate documentary, artistic, corporate, and amateur photography from one another but rather would treat them as interlinking systems of image classes. And just as the industrial photograph and the advertisement are ideological, so too all photography must be understood not as a form of realism or as a hierarchy of better or worse artistic expressions but as the concretization of social values.

Photography thereby becomes a branch of social and intellectual history. Using photographs as interpretations of the world rather than misunderstanding them as windows on the past, historians can analyze the social construction of reality. Photographs can exemplify Berger and Luckmann's sociology of knowledge, which posits ideology as a form of belief that appears in societies without monolithic interpretations of the world. They write that "the distinctiveness of ideology is . . . that the same overall universe is interpreted in different ways, depending upon concrete vested interests within society."[9] This statement does not go far enough, however, since it suggests that each vested interest will develop only one ideology as a form of self-legitimation. General Electric created multiple legitimations of itself, addressing each to an appropriate group. Large corporations generate not a hegemonic ideology but rather plural identities. If legally still defined as individuals, in practice corporations have not been unitary.

Works in American studies and history have scarcely recognized this multiplicity. As a result many continue to search for definitions of the worker or the meaning of a new process such as the assembly line, which is to say that they fundamentally misunderstand twentieth-century culture. Today no object of study, including the individual, can be conceived as a unity.[10] Moreover each of the contradictory identities given to the fragments of a subject has itself been partially shaped through public relations and advertising. Photographs from General Electric provide only one illustration of this disassembled historical subject. Study of other coporate forms of representation, such as commercial art or television, would disclose a similar deployment of image worlds.

The disintegration of the subject in corporate photography registers a widespread transformation in American culture as a whole between 1900 and 1930. In other fields it found expression as the multiplication of perspectives in cubism, the use of several narrators in experimental literature, and the professionalization of university teaching. In every area it became more difficult to work from a single perspective as social reality became problematic. General Electric expressed that transformation through the diverse points of view taken up by its corporate cameras. Ultimately it was not any particular ideology that mattered, since those for managers, workers, engineers, and consumers contradicted one another. Rather the ideological effect of this multiplication of image worlds mattered as the corporation became an ungraspable interplay of conflicting truths, each of which it validated. The multiple perspectives of a cubist painting or the several points of view of a modernist novel occur within a single text, making fragmentation visible and reintegration possible. But the corporation provided no privileged space outside the welter of conflicting views where a reader could understand the larger pattern. To glimpse the variety of realities the corporation constructed is to see the insubstantiality of every photograph. And ironically that very disintegration of meaning made each separate image world more attractive.

Notes

Chapter 1

1. A handful of studies were very important in conceptualizing this book, and I would like to acknowledge them here since they are not often cited in the text. John F. Kasson's *Amusing the Million* (New York: Hill & Wang, 1978) first showed how useful photographs could be in historical studies. Susan Sontag's *On Photography* (New York: Delta Books, 1977) further excited my interest, although in the process of my research I gradually rejected most of her views. Two books had the greatest value: Barbara Rosenblum's *Photographers at Work* (New York: Holmes and Meier, 1978) and Pierre Bourdieu's *Un Art Moyen: essai sur les usages sociaux de la photographie* (Paris: Les Editions de Minuit, 1965). No one working on photography in society can afford to ignore these two fine studies. Finally, I also found Jack Hurley's pioneering *Industry and the Photographic Image* (New York: Dover Publications, 1980) a useful survey of the field.

2. Henry Nash Smith, *Virgin Land* (Cambridge: Harvard University Press, 1950); R. W. B. Lewis, *The American Adam* (Chicago: University of Chicago Press, 1955); Leo Marx, *The Machine in the Garden* (New York: Oxford University Press, 1965); John William Ward, *Andrew Jackson: Symbol for an Age* (New York: Oxford University Press, 1955); Barbara Novak, *Nature and Culture: American Landscape and Painting* (New York: Oxford University Press, 1980).

3. Bruce Kuklik, "Myth and Symbol in American Studies," *American Quarterly* 24 (October 1972): 435–450.

4. Herbert Gutman, one of the leading practitioners of the new social history, to his credit early detected the weaknesses inherent within it, decrying the balkanizing tendencies already evident by 1977. See his *Work, Culture, and Society* (New York: Vintage Books, 1977), p. xii. Among more recent critics, see Gordon Wood, "Star Spangled History," *New York Review of Books*, August 12, 1982.

5. John Winthrop Hammond, *Men and Volts* (Philadelphia: J. B. Lippincott, 1941).

6. Thomas P. Hughes, *Networks of Power: Electrification in Western Society, 1880–1930* (Baltimore: Johns Hopkins University Press, 1983). For an extended review, see David E. Nye, "Writing the History of Technology," *Science, Technology and Human Values* (Spring 1984).

Chapter 2

1. John Winthrop Hammond, "The Psychology of a Nation's Wants," Hammond Papers, General Electric Plant Library, Schenectady, L 5141. All subsequent references to the Hammond Papers will use the abbreviation HP, followed by the file reference number. Bruce Barton quotation provided to the author by George Wise, company historian, General Electric.

2. A good overview of early development in the electrical field is C. Mackechnie Jarvis's "The Rise of the Electrical Industry," in *A History of Technology*, ed. Charles Singer et al. (New York: Oxford University Press, 1955), 5: 177–234. The relationship between this early work and the American electrical companies is discussed in Arthur A. Bright's *The Electric-Lamp Industry: Technological Change and Economic Development from 1800 to 1947* (New York: Macmillan, 1949), passim, and in Harold C. Passer's *The Electrical Manufacturers, 1875–1900.* (Cambridge: Harvard University Press, 1953), esp. chaps. 5, 7, 9, 13. One recent article by Thomas P. Hughes is of exceptional value: "The Electrification of America: The System Builders," *Technology and Culture* 20, no. 1 (January 1979): 125.

3. Jarvis, "Rise of the Electrical Industry," pp. 210–211.

4. Matthew Josephson, *Edison: A Biography* (New York: McGraw-Hill, 1959), p. 178.

5. Ibid., pp. 189, 203.

6. Passer, *Electrical Manufacturers*, p. 362.

7. Ibid., pp. 102–103.

8. Ibid., p. 150.

9. Ibid., pp. 52–56.

10. Ibid., p. 325.

11. Ibid., pp. 329–334.

12. Alfred D. Chandler, *The Visible Hand: The Managerial Revolution in American Business* (Cambridge: Harvard University Press, 1977), p. 426.

13. *Professional Management in General Electric* (New York: General Electric Company, 1953), vol. 1.

14. Ibid., p. 13.

15. Executive correspondence, 1897, HP-L5900.

16. In particular, see Edward Bellamy's utopian novel, *Looking Backward*, which achieved a huge popular success in the 1880s and led to the formation of many Nationalist Clubs working for socialism.

17. Mulford Q. Sibley, *Political Ideas and Ideologies: A History of Political Thought* (New York: Harper & Row, 1970), p. 526.

18. Hammond, "Psychology," HP-L5148.

19. Covert, political public relations is the subject of chapter 8.

20. Chandler, *Visible Hand*, pp. 224–226, 289–299; Daniel Boorstin, *The Americans: The Democratic Experience* (New York: Random House, 1973), pp. 137–146.

21. Josephson, *Edison*, pp. 166–168, 244–245.

22. Thomas A. Edison, "Dangers of Electric Lighting," *North American Review* (November 1889).

23. Thomas P. Hughes, "Harold P. Brown and the Execution's Current: An Incident in the AC-DC Controversy," *Business History Review* 32 (1958): 143–166.

24. Alan Raucher, *Public Relations and Business, 1900–1929* (Baltimore: Johns Hopkins Press), p. 8.

25. Ibid., pp. 9–10.

26. Ibid., p. 6. Also see Raucher's discussion of the utilities and public relations in chap. 4, particularly pp. 60–63.

27. Gabriel Kolko, *The Triumph of Conservatism: A Reinterpretation of American History, 1900–1916* (Chicago: Quadrangle Books, 1963); Robert Weibe, *The Search for Order, 1877–1920* (New York: Hill and Wang, 1967). This is not to say that Weibe and Kolko agree on all points but only to point to the general thrust of their arguments, which tended to debunk the muckraker view of the trusts.

28. Hollis Townsend, *A History of NELA Park, 1911–1957* (Cleveland: General Electric Company, 1957), p. 9 (copy in the library of the Schenectady plant).

29. Ibid., p. 10.

30. Ibid., p. 11. Bright, *Electric-Lamp Industry*, confirms Townsend's figures and provides further statistics that show how thoroughly General Electric and NELA dominated incandescent lamp production. In 1910 the national market was divided as follows: General Electric, 42 percent; NELA, 38 percent; Westinghouse, 13 percent; all others, 7 percent. See pp. 150–152.

31. Paul W. Keating, *Lamps for a Brighter America: A History of the General Electric Lamp Business* (New York: McGraw-Hill, 1954), pp. 85–86.

32. Ibid., pp. 89–96. Also see chapter 8. After 1911 the NELA in Cleveland served as a research and marketing center, while another organization with the same acronym and a very similar membership later grew powerful in the public relations of electrification.

33. David Loth, *Swope of G.E.* (New York: Simon & Schuster, 1958), pp. 121–122.

34. D. M. Diggs, "The Entering Wedge," *General Electric Digest* 2 (July–August 1922): 9.

35. Forest MacDonald, *Insull* (Chicago: University of Chicago Press, 1962), pp. 67–71.

36. "Electricity in the Homes of the United States," *General Electric Digest* 5 (April 1925): 30–32. And see John Winthrop Hammond, *Men and Volts: The Story of General Electric* (Philadelphia and London: J. B. Lippincott, 1941), pp. 229–240, 254–258, 285–298. Hammond's work was a heavily edited in-house history that was only nominally published by Lippincott. The manuscript had been completed in the early 1930s, but the company refused to publish it or any other history of itself until the end of the depression, for reasons never stated publicly. Hammond's volume is invaluable on technical matters and in providing an overview. Regrettably some of his chapters on welfare capitalism

were excised. I thank Thomas Hughes who discussed the sequence of electrification with me briefly in the fall of 1981.

37. MacDonald, *Insull*, p. 104.

38. Ibid., pp. 99–100.

39. "Major Appliance Business," HP-K-4762.

40. Information and notes on this meeting supplied by George Wise, General Electric company historian. The meeting is also described in Loth, *Swope*, p. 142.

41. Ibid. (Wise).

42. Bruce Barton, *The Man Nobody Knows* (Indianapolis: Bobbs Merrill, 1924).

43. Wise, notes.

44. HP L 5145–5148.

45. Ibid., 5149.

46. G. Emerson Markham, "Behind the WGY Farm Broadcasts, Goes the Message of the Electrification Program," *Monogram* (July 1930): 18. The Hammond Papers also contain considerable materials on the early history of radio. See particularly the historical overview from 1883 to the late 1920s prepared by Harry Schroeder and used by W. C. White, HP-L 4303–4313. On WGY in particular see HP-4332–4350, L 3480.

47. Hammond, HP L-5144.

48. Barton, *Man*, pp. 140–141.

49. The *General Electric Review* began in 1903 and continued until 1949.

50. *Works News* began in 1917 and lasted, with one year's interruption, until 1938.

Chapter 3

1. For the predecessors of photography, see Gisele Freund, *Photography and Society* (Boston: David Godine, 1980), chap. 1. There is no entirely satisfactory history of photography at present. Helmut Gernsheim's works were marred by three problems: excessive attention to great men and all that that implies in a historical work; too narrow a cultural focus, his work dealing almost entirely with England, France, Germany, and to a lesser extent the United States; and too little attention to the social impact of photography. Still his *The History of Photography, 1685–1914* (New York: McGraw-Hill, 1969) remains a landmark work, along with Beaumont Newhall's *The History of Photography from 1838 to the Present Day* (New York: Museum of Modern Art, and Simon & Schuster, 1949), which shares the virtues of painstaking research found in Gernsheim, with the noted defects.

2. Robert Taft, *Photography and the American Scene* (1938; New York: Dover, 1964), pp. 138–152. For the history of photographic companies, see Reese Jenkins, *Images and Enterprise: Technology and the American Photographic Industry: 1839–1925* (Baltimore: Johns Hopkins University Press, 1976).

3. Novak, *Nature and Culture*, pp. 177–178.

4. On the development of corporations and their relationship to the emerging mass market of the late nineteenth century, see Alan Trachtenberg, *The Incorporation of America* (New York: McGraw-Hill, 1982), pp. 129–139.

5. Taft, *Photography*, pp. 430–435.

6. Ibid., p. 436; William M. Ivins, *Prints and Visual Communication* (Cambridge: MIT Press, 1969), pp. 126–130.

7. Raymond Smith Schuneman, "The Photograph in Print: An Examination of New York Daily Newspapers, 1890–1937" (Ph.D. diss., University of Minnesota, 1966), pp. 97–100.

8. Frank Luther Mott, "The Magazine Revolution and Popular Ideas in the Nineties," in Abraham S. Eisenstadt, *American History: Recent Interpretations* (New York: Thomas Crowell Company, 1969), 2: 218–232.

9. These and many other house organs can be examined in the Baker Library at Harvard University.

10. Taft, *Photography*, p. 61.

11. *Able's Photographic Weekly* began publication in Cleveland, Ohio, in 1908 under the editorship of Charles and Juan Able, selling for five cents an issue, or one dollar and fifty cents a year.

12. Ibid. 7 (1911): 11.

13. Photography House interior and exterior views, negative numbers 752e and 751e, respectively, from the General Electric Photographic Archives, hereafter cited as GEPA. The only published source available to scholars is David E. Nye, *A Catalogue of the General Electric Photographic Archives, 1890–1940* (Schenectady: General Electric Company, 1981). This catalog lists 7,000 representative photographs divided into the following six categories: industrial photographs, the American scene, General Electric products, advertising and public relations, inventors and executives, and General Electric overseas. The volume is indexed with references both to specific subjects and to their geographical location.

14. *Works News*, September 5, 1924. Copy also in HP-L 1256. This is an invaluable article.

15. Statistics based on personal inspection of the present collection, which is housed at the General Electric Plant in Schenectady, New York. Negatives were numbered consecutively, reaching a total of over 250,000 by 1919. The negatives have not been preserved; what remains are the 8 × 10 master prints made from them before they were destroyed in 1916–1917, presumably because they took up a great deal of space. After 1920 glass plates were seldom used, with the result that negatives were less bulky and easier to store. These negatives are still preserved but are not organized.

16. *Works News*, September 5, 1924, p. 18.

17. Ibid. Also see ibid., December 1917, p. 5, which contains the following information: "Nearly 200 members of the Publicity Bureau celebrated the 20th anniversary of the department at the Schenectady Boat Club. . . . Today there are 242 [employees], not including the representatives at the various works and offices of the Company."

18. *Professional Management in General Electric*, pp. 18–19.

19. Circular letter, HP L 5900. Copies went to all vice-presidents, department managers, factory managers, and others.

20. *Works News*, December 1917, p. 5.

21. Information in the following paragraphs from an interview with Ralph Carrano, November 19, 1981.

22. Information about the photographic department obtained in an interview with Paul Sorell, November 19, 1981. Sorell worked for the photographic department for thirty-three years beginning in 1938, starting at the bottom and working up to the supervisory level. He knew many of the individuals who had been with the department in the previous decades.

23. Listings of the negative numbers and one line descriptions of these and many other photographs can be found in Nye, *Catalogue*, pp. 1–9–1–17.

24. *Commercial Photographer* began publication in 1925 as an offshoot of the publishers of *Able's*. W. H. Sanderson, "Photography in the GMC Truck Plant," *Commercial Photographer* 3 (December 1928): 109. Charles Able, "Commercial Photography at the Edgewood Arsenal," *Commercial Photographer* 3 (January 1928): 155–158. See also Able, "Photography at the Goodyear Factories," *Commercial Photographer* 2 (March 1927): 245.

25. Sanderson, *Photography*, p. 110. For more information on commercial and industrial photography in the early years, see J. Deschin, "Photography in the Ads: Behind the Scenes," *Scientific American* 152 (April 1935): 175; F. C. Ellis, "Photography Works for Industry," *Scientific American* 149 (August 1933): 70; N. Haz, "Commercial Photography of Today," *American Photography* 28 (December 1934): 723–732; W. J. Shaw, "Camera's Part in Making Profits," *Factory and Industrial Management* 76 (September 1928): 495.

26. George W. Hance, a successful commercial photographer from Northampton, Massachusetts, published a long series of articles during 1913 in *Able's Photographic Weekly* under the auspices of the Commercial Federation of the Photographer's Association of America. These articles, divided into twenty chapters, comprise a virtual summary of the field at that date, starting with cameras in chapter 1, lenses and prisms in chapter 2, and thereafter plates, interiors, store windows, homes and gardens, and so on through all the various kinds of images the commercial photographer ordinarily had to make as part of his business. He included sections on combination prints, doctoring negatives, prices, and prints, and virtually everything else a novice would need to know in order to enter the field. These chapters ran from late spring 1913 (vol. 13) until the following year (through vols. 14 and 15). Hereafter all references will be made to the chapters of this work rather than to the issue of the magazine. Hance's articles were profusely illustrated, the photographs serving not only as evidence of his ability and as examples of varying commercial genres but also providing a visible text for him to comment upon. This quotation comes from chapter 1, vol. 13, p. 511.

27. Ibid., chap. 2, pp. 533–543.

28. Ibid., chap. 1, p. 513.

29. "Photographing Machinery in Position," *Wilson's Photographic Magazine* 48 (March 1911): 129.

30. Hance, chap. 14, p. 411 (in vol. 14).

31. "Photographing Machinery," p. 130.

32. Hance, chap. 14, p. 412, includes an illustration that required forty-five minutes of exposure time. Similarly long exposures with small aperture openings were typical.

33. Ibid., p. 411, plate 3, neg. 6343.

34. Ibid., chap. 10, p. 256. In the following chapter Hance described another technique for use with glass: blowing by means of an airbrush "a solution of blue Diamond Dye dissolved in gum arabic." This coated a glass object with a "light dust, the color of robin's egg blue, which photographs white and does not reflect." Plate 4, *Domestic Range*, neg. 291976.

35. Ibid., chap. 3, p. 557.

36. Ibid., pp. 559–560, plate 5, neg. 217877.

37. Ibid., chap. 6, p. 531 (in vol. 14), plate 6, neg. 387107.

38. Ibid., chap. 18, p. 486.

39. Roman Gubern, *Mensajes Iconicos en la Cultura de Masas* (Barcelona: Editorial Luman, 1974), pp. 52–54. His chapter on photography is astute and deserves far more attention than it has received.

40. Quoted in Mary Douglas, ed., *Rules and Meaning* (London: Penguin Books, 1973), p. 62.

41. Louis Hjelmslev, *Language, an Introduction* (Madison: University of Wisconsin Press, 1970), pp. 32–44.

42. Roman Jakobson, "Linguistics and Poetics," in Thomas Sebeok, *Style in Language* (Cambridge: MIT Press, 1960), p. 353.

43. Eco, *A Theory of Semiotics* (Bloomington: Indiana University Press, 1979), p. 141. I would like to thank Thomas Sebeok and particularly Paul Bouissac for discussing the Jakobson model with me.

44. This process closely resembles the way newspapers handle their photographic work; see Rosenblum, *Photographers*.

45. Edward Weston, *The Daybooks of Edward Weston*, 2 vols. (New York: Aperture, 1973), and *The Flame of Recognition*, ed. Beaumont Newhall (New York: Aperture, 1971).

46. Discussions occurred during the summer of 1980 when I worked as a consultant with the photographic department at General Electric for three months. These were not interviews but participant observers' discussions with staff as they went about their work. As it happened, this also included a photographic session in which the author's own picture was taken for use in a company publication, the *Monogram* (June 1980) back cover.

47. This kind of communication is not unprecedented. See, for example, Paul Bouissac's *Circus and Culture: A Semiotic Approach* (Bloomington: University of Indiana Press, 1976), which examines, among many other coding systems at work in a circus performance, animal acts where two different coding systems "function simultaneously and independently during a performance: the training code, which ensures effective communication between the trainer and the animal, and the code of the act, which permits communication between the performer and the audience" (p. 52). In the strictest sense, the creation of a photographic message involves even more codes than have

been indicated, including that between the editor and the photographer, that used in the developing room, that used in the layout of the magazine where the photograph appears, and that of the viewer of the image when it appears. Investigation of all these, however, is precluded by the lack of evidence, and even were it possible, the benefits of such a detailed investigation would perhaps not be worth the considerable space necessary to describe it. Here the focus is on the work of the photographer since the other stages in image processing were much more routinized, as in the mechanized developing process.

48. Roland Barthes, *Image, Music, Text* (New York: Hill and Wang, 1977), p. 17. In the same volume, Barthes states: "In the photograph—at least at the level of the literal message—the relationship of signifieds to signifiers is not one of 'transformation' but of 'recording,' and the absence of a code clearly reinforces the myth of photographic 'naturalness': the scene is *there*, captured mechanically, not humanly (the mechanical is here a guarantee of objectivity)" (p. 44). I disagree with this approach.

49. Roland Barthes, *Mythologies* (New York: Hill and Wang, 1972), pp. 116–117.

50 Rosenblum, "Style as Social Process," *American Sociological Review* 43: 432–435.

51. M. Andre, "Classy Not Classical," *Art News* 74 (November 1975).

52. Lewis Hine photograph, "The Boss Teaches a Young Spinner in a North Carolina Cotton Mill" (Hine's title), is a good example of documentary reform-minded photography at its best. For a discussion of the differences between his work and that of corporate photographers, with particular regard to industrial accidents, see David E. Nye, "Ideology in Photography," in *American Studies in Transition* (Odense, Denmark: Odense University Press, 1985). Also see Alan Trachtenberg's important essay, "Camera Work: Notes toward an Investigation," *Massachusetts Review* 19 (1978): 834–859.

53. See Nye, *Catalogue* 11, particularly photographs: 12260e Olympia Mills, Columbia South Carolina; 224377e Henderson Cotton Mill, North Carolina; 12037e New Orleans Cotton Mills. Using the General Electric collection, one can trace the electrification of various industries from about 1895 to World War II.

Chapter 4

1. David P. Forsyth, *The Business Press in America, 1750–1865* (Philadelphia: Chilton Books, 1964), pp. 16–20. The indispensable background work for any study of American magazines is Frank Luther Mott's *A History of American Magazines* published in four volumes by Harvard University Press, 1957, covering together 1741 to 1905. Useful as a supplement and completion of Mott's work is Theodore Peterson's *Magazines in the Twentieth Century* (Urbana: University of Illinois Press, 1964). Also see the special issue on magazines of the *Journal of American Culture* 3 (Spring 1980).

2. Forsyth, *Business Press*, pp. 25–33.

3. Ibid., chaps. 1, 2 passim. Julien Elfenbein's *Business Journalism* (reprint;

New York: Greenwood Press, 1969), pp. 301–309, contains a useful list of business publications that appeared before 1900, in chronological order of appearance.

4. The first upsurge of the workers' movement in the United States coincided with the politics of Jacksonianism, which Arthur Schlesinger chronicled in his *The Age of Jackson* (Boston: Little, Brown, 1945). Schlesinger tended to interpret the mechanics movement in the terms appropriate to the coalitions of the New Deal. More recent scholars have discounted the labor movement's strength and its existence as a class phenomenon. For discussion of these issues, see Edward Pessen, *Jacksonian America: Society, Personality, and Politics* (Chicago: Dorsey Press, 1969), and the same author's *The Many-Faceted Jacksonian Era: New Interpretations* (Westport, Conn.: Greenwood Press, 1977).

5. Elfenbein, *Business Journalism*, pp. 157–159.

6. David W. Noble, *America by Design* (New York: Oxford University Press, 1979), points out that the corporations did engage in large-scale educational programs, however. General Electric in particular ran a well-known test course at both its Schenectady and Lynn works, training college graduates in the latest engineering. Just over half of the graduates of this course remained with the company after it was over. The situation is comparable to that in many computer companies today, which have had to train many people to meet their rapidly developing needs. But like the electrical corporations at the turn of the century, they too wish to shift this job to the universities.

7. Ibid., pp. 39–40.

8. Edwin T. Layton, Jr., *The Revolt of the Engineers: Social Responsibility and the American Engineering Profession* (Cleveland: Case Western Reserve University Press, 1971).

9. The connection between electric motors and the advent of the assembly line was personal as well as logical. Henry Ford was an admirer and later a friend of Edison, whom he visited at his iron ore mining project in the 1890s. The project was automated, including the first use of rubber conveyor belts, which Edison developed jointly with their official inventor, Thomas Robbins. On the Ford-Edison connection, see David E. Nye, *Henry Ford: Ignorant Idealist* (Port Washington, N.Y.: Kennikat Press, 1979). On the Edison iron mining project, see Theodore Waters, "Edison's Revolution in Iron Mining," *McClure's Magazine* (November 1897). Statistics on electrification from Nathan Rosenberg, *Technology and American Economic Growth* (New York: Harper & Row, 1972), p. 162.

10. Elfenbein, *Business Journalism*, pp. 185–187, briefly describes the emergence of electrical trade publications. Like the corporations themselves, these merged many times between 1880 and 1900.

11. *General Electric Review*, March 2, 1903, p. 1. On the second page confidentiality was stressed again: "The Sales Committee instructed the Publication Bureau to prepare and issue this periodical for the exclusive information and assistance of the Company's agents."

12. Ibid., p. 2.

13. Statement based on sampling of issues from 1910, 1915, 1920, 1925, and 1930. Photographic classes during these years were also checked and found to remain unchanged in style and in proportional distribution.

14. Editorial in the *Review* 9, nos. 1–2 (January 1908). Sample topics taken from the same issue.

15. Editorial in ibid. 13, nos. 1, 3 (January 1910). Although the *Review* dealt with electrification projects abroad, as in an article on France (vol. 29, no. 7), such articles never predominated. Statistics from Rosenberg, *Technology*, p. 157.

16. This statistic arrived at through analysis of random issues in the 1920s and 1930s. Class 1 represented 62 percent; class 2, 9 percent; class 3, 4 percent; class 4, 4 percent; and class 5, 3 percent (classes in order of presentation).

17. In the General Electric Archives as a whole this class accounts for at least half of the more than 1 million photographs. This class represented by three images: plate 3, shown in chapter 2; plate 9, "Arc Welder Generator Direct Connected to Induction Motor," neg. 318506; and plate 10, "300 Amp. 12000 Volt Electrically Operated Oil Switch." Similar images were common throughout American technical publications; today plastic white tables are used to achieve the apparent isolation of smaller machines. Photographers can also paint out the background, as was probably done in the case of plate 9.

18. This class represented by two images: neg. 10826, an unidentified power generating station; and neg. 3999079, "Indiana and Michigan Electric Co., Fort Wayne, Ind. Type H-60-3333-C-132000-34650D Transformer High Voltage Side."

19. Three images represent this class: neg. 475 (not shown), of a motor, from the period when labels were not yet affixed to images. Yet even at this time a man is used for scale, and the machine is isolated from its surroundings. Neg. 399061 does not name or even mention the seven men around "2(WC)-60-220000 Y-66000 Y-11000 Transformer in Testing Pit." Neg. 480591 similarly ignores the two men before the "19th Stage Bucket Wheel for G.E. Steam Turbine, Assembled for Factory Inspection. For Brooklyn Edison Co."

20. Neg. 106234 portrays Willis R. Whitney, for many years a leading scientist at the General Electric Laboratory. The black background and the soft focus of this picture are typical.

21. No group portraits have been reproduced because they are so undistinguished as to be easily imagined: a line of men, standing formally on steps, near a wall, or in front of a building. The camera was placed just far enough to include every face and frame the group as a whole but with no insistence on getting the entire body or on conveying the surrounding context, which is usually impossible to identify.

22. See note 16.

23. Weston's work is discussed in Newhall, *History*, and many other works, including A. D. Coleman's *Light Readings* (New York: Oxford University Press, 1979), which contains a representative repudiation: "Edward Weston, of course, is fifteen years dead, and his work is a decreasingly active influence on young photographers. . . . The 'purism' he advocated is creatively inhibiting and so closely linked to a particular subject matter, style, and camera format as to negate large segments of the photographic vocabulary and eliminate broad areas of experience from the photographer's imagistic concerns"

(pp. 189–190). It is ironic that Weston's work can also be compared to an even harsher purism than his own, practiced at General Electric, revaluing his work more positively than is possible for those who are struggling to throw him off as an influence in art photography.

24. On the camera work of pictorialism, see John Wallace Gillies, *Principles of Pictorial Photography* (New York: Arno Press Reprint, 1973), and H. P. Robinson, *The Elements of a Pictorial Photograph* (New York: Arno Press Reprint, 1973). For the darkroom methods of pictorialism, see William Crawford, *The Keepers of Light* (Dobbs Ferry, New York: Morgan & Morgan, 1979), pp. 85–97, 199–226.

25. On precisionism see Abraham A. Davidson, *Early American Modernist Painting, 1910–1935* (New York: Harper & Row), pp. 182–225.

Chapter 5

1. Edison's early research laboratory preserved the work rhythms of artisanal labor, as described by E. P. Thompson in "Time, Work Discipline, and Industrial Capitalism," *Past and Present* 38 (1967): 72–74. On application to Edison at Menlo Park, see Nye, *The Invented Self* (Odense, 1983), pp. 75–84. Neg. 109776, "Interior View of Edison's Laboratory Menlo Park, N.J. Feb. 22, 1880, Showing Edison and his principal Assistants."

2. Neg. 651, from third volume of the General Electric Archives. Neg. CD 2382e, "Punch and Die Department, 1901," from about seven years later, shows a greater formality in overall design, although the individuals still pose themselves, while neg. CD2380e shows "Women working in wire and cable department, Building 14," exhibiting the greatest formality of any of these early images.

3. The facile assumption that women were passive at work sites has undergone considerable revision in recent years as a result of careful case studies, such as Tamara K. Hareven's *Amoskeag* (New York: Pantheon Books, 1978) and her "Family Work Patterns of Immigrant Laborers in a Planned Industrial Town, 1900–1930," *Journal of Urban History* 1 (1975). Her work and that of Virginia Yans-McLaughlin have emphasized the family as a flexible institution that adjusted quite differently in each factory town to the peculiarities of each industry. Cotton mills could employ the entire family, for example, while steel plants hired almost exclusively men. General Electric fell between these two extremes, hiring in Schenectady between 10 and 15 percent of its work force as women during prosperous years. Most of these women were unmarried, and the company exhibited a paternalistic concern for them in establishing women's clubs, a single-sex summer camp, and health care facilities for them.

4. "The Schenectady Plant," *Electrical World* 6 (1888).

5. Compare engraving A53621, "View of the main floor of the wire insulating department, No. 1 shop," with CD-2380, "Wire and Cable Department, Second Floor of Building 14, Schenectady Works." Plates 22 and 23 have neg. numbers 12077 and 12078, respectively, another piece of evidence that they were taken at the same time. For an example of the industrial landscape as it later developed in images for managers, see plate 38, in which the camera has

been raised to a higher perspective, and plates 39 and 40 where workers serve as anonymous parts of the factory.

6. This transformation was only partly a matter of changes in scale. Bigger companies, as current Japanese plants make clear, are not necessarily impersonal. No detailed study of General Electric workers at the Schenectady plant exists, but John T. Cumber has done an admirable study. His *Working Class Community in Industrial America* (Westport, Conn.: Greenwood Press, 1979) describes how General Electric's Lynn plant "transformed the work pattern, and ultimately the very community, of the workers. . . . General Electric workers did not work together in small cooperating groups. The structure of the plant and the demands of the jobs isolated them from the informal socializing of the shoe workers." (p. 223), who provide Cumber with a useful counterpoint. Welfare capitalism was a logical and necessary response to the breakdown of worker communities under the pressure of the new workplace.

7. An excellent set of statistics on the growth of General Electric may be found in *Professional Management in General Electric*, pp. 6–19.

8. See Stanley Aronowitz, *False Promises: The Shaping of American Working Class Consciousness* (New York: McGraw-Hill, 1973), pp. 148–149.

9. By 1917 meters were assembled at Fort Wayne plant by women on an assembly line, as can be seen in photographs taken at the time, neg. 282106e (not reproduced).

10. In the early 1900s the corporation produced a series of twelve images recording the manufacture of electric light bulbs, the work done entirely by young women; neg. 185459e–185470e (not reproduced).

11. Larry Hart, *Schenectady's Golden Era, 1880–1930* (Schenectady, N.Y.: Old Dorp Books, 1974), p. 291. Attendance figures for schools in Schenectady City Reports for the 1920s. Poles and Italians were the largest ethnic groups, followed by a great many others.

12. Thompson, "Time," p. 73; Herbert Gutman, *Work, Culture and Society in Industrializing America* (New York: Vintage Books, 1977), pp. 3–78, esp. pp. 36–47.

13. Elihu Thompson's newspaper file, now in the Lynn Historical Society, contains a series of clippings from 1892 describing a strike in which workers demanded a nine-hour day, six days a week, and received a compromise, a two-hour reduction from fifty-eight to fifty-six hours per week settlement.

14. See Hart, *Schenectady's Golden Era*, pp. 9–14; Kathryn Rich, "George R. Lunn: Socialist Mayor of Schenectady" (typescript, Schenectady County Public Library, 1966); Kenneth E. Hendrickson, "George R. Lunn and the Socialist Era in Schenectady, New York, 1909–1916," *New York History* 42 (January 1966).

15. Hart, *Schenectady's Golden Era*, p. 13. In the Schenectady city hall historical collection is a newspaper scrapbook containing Lunn's own clippings from the period he was mayor. They provide an invaluable body of information.

16. Quotation appears in Ronald W. Schatz, *The Electrical Workers: A History of Labor at General Electric and Westinghouse, 1923–60* (Urbana: University of Illinois, 1983), p. 37. Schatz's chapter 2 is useful background.

17. On the fear of "reds," see Robert K. Murray's *Red Scare: A Study in*

National Hysteria (New York: McGraw-Hill, 1964); on socialism, see John Laslett, *Labor and the Left: A Study of Socialist and Radical Influences in the American Labor Movement, 1881–1924* (New York: Basic Books, 1970).

18. The following are only a sample: "Teaching Americanism in the Factory," in *Literary Digest* 60 (February 1919): 28–9, makes some reference to the Ford plants in a general discussion; H. B. Alexander editorialized on "Americanization" in *The Nation* 109 (September 1919): 367–9; Jane Addams questioned the idea in "Nationalism, a Dogma?" in *Survey* 43 (February 1920): 524–526; and there were more than 75 other articles between 1918 and 1922, the majority in the first two years.

19. Peter Roberts, *The Problem of Americanization* (New York: MacMillan & Co., 1920), p. 212. Also see p. 99.

20. E. W. Rice was a powerful executive within General Electric who had been instrumental in creating the General Electric Research Laboratories in 1901 and who later helped to form the National Industrial Conference Board in 1915.

21. Edward George Hartmann's *The Movement to Americanize the Immigrant* (New York: Columbia University Press, 1948) remains an indispensable source. Hartmann traces the development of Americanization from the 1890s on, beginning as voluntary and cooperative efforts. Quotation from p. 212. On Schenectady mass meeting for Americanization in 1913, see U.S. Bureau of Naturalization, *Report of the Commissioner of Naturalization*, 1917, pp. 533–534.

22. Stuart Brandes, *American Welfare Capitalism* (Chicago: University of Chicago Press, 1976). Also see David Brody, "The Rise and Decline of Welfare Capitalism," in John Breaman, ed., *Change and Continuity in the Twentieth Century: The 1920's* (Columbus: Ohio State University Press, 1968); and Richard Edwards, *Contested Terrain* (New York: Basic Books, 1979), pp. 85–97. Welfare capitalism was compatible with but not identical to scientific management; see Samuel Haber, *Efficiency and Uplift: Scientific Management in the Progressive Era, 1890–1920* (Chicago: University of Chicago Press, 1964).

23. Charles M. Ripley, *Life in a Large Manufacturing Plant* (Schenectady: General Electric Company, 1919), and *Romance of a Great Factory* (Schenectady: General Electric Company, 1919). Both volumes are illustrated with photographs taken by company photographers.

24. Robert W. Bruere describes the employee representation plan at "West Lynn," in *Survey*, April 1, 1926. The plan can also be reconstructed from the *Lynn Works News*, an edition of which can be found in the Lynn Public Library.

25. "What Employee Publications Are Doing to Improve Industrial Relations," *Industrial Management* 59 (April 1925): 213. On company magazines, also see Jean Atherton Flexner, "Selling the Company," *New Republic*, April 9, 1924, pp. 171–174.

26. Charles Steinmetz, "Comments on Bolshevism and Labor Unions," *Works News*, April 11, 1919, p. 6.

27. "Employee Publications," p. 214.

28. On circulations: in 1925, the *New Republic*'s circulation was just under 37,000, the *Survey Graphic*'s, 23,100. Combined they reached fewer persons

than the *Works News*, which went to each of the company's more than 71,000 workers. The *New Republic* was printed on poor-quality paper and carried no photographs. *Survey Graphic* carried photographs, but they were poorly reproduced. Moreover, in the 1920s the *Graphic* had lost some of the influence it earlier held in the field of sociology as a whole, which had become more professionalized, imitating hard sciences in their use of statistics. Photographs, once common in the *American Sociological Review*, had almost entirely disappeared from it at this date. Their policy reflected a general aversion to photographs in the most academic journals, leaving image control in the hands of the large corporations.

29. The formats of the company worker magazines also varied somewhat, that at Lynn having somewhat fewer photographs. It did not have as large a photographic staff to draw upon. Analysis is valid for both.

30. See neg. 463283, "Bearing shell being babbitted. Building 16, Schenectady Works"; neg. 114658, "Crane Follower in Motor Department Directing Load to be Raised"; neg. 551409, "Model G-E Switchboard Assembled to symbolically illustrate craftsmanship of G.E. switchboard builders," original caption affixed by the photographic department; and neg. 241203, "Woman operating vertical milling machine in railway motor department, Building 5, Erie Works." No photographs of this type can be found in the collection before 1917. Note that workers are not named, even when being isolated as individuals.

31. No images of assembly line workers ever appeared on the cover.

32. The activities of the teams were carefully chronicled in the *Works News*, and the sports section included more personal names than any other part of the magazine. While there were more teams in summer than in winter, basketball, football, boxing, rowing, bowling, and baseball were all encouraged. On a few occasions champions from one plant played those of another, particularly in the case of Lynn and Schenectady. See plate 28, "Accounting Basketball Team, 1924," neg. 121670.

33. Neg. 135416, "Bowling team—Bloomfield Works"; neg. 112302, "Girls in Motor Department, Fourth Floor of Building 40, Schenectady Works, wearing woman-alls." Note that they have been isolated against a white background in the same way that photographs usually treated machines for the *General Electric Review*.

34. See Nye, *Catalogue*, pp. 2–29; neg. 822045, "Six Stefanowicz sisters with wartime production awards, G.E. Erie Works, 1943."

35. Neg. 439786, "Americanization Activity—Boccie Bowling at noon recess period beside building 68"; neg. 425653, "Americanization class in English, Bldg. 40—Teacher H. Axford." This last is a typical example of a whole class of images, each made of a class at work. Invariably the men are in groups of three to seven, seated at their work tables, books in hand. The teacher almost always stands behind them, dressed as a white-collar employee. Often, as here, the workers give various signs of unease.

36. Neg. 408916, "Americanization Class in Civics, preparing for citizenship," and 444217, "Americanization Class in Civics, two additional students," show the men dressed better than in their language class photographs. For enacting the "Drama of U.S. Congress" in class (neg. 421611) they were better

dressed yet, and in images taken in the courtroom itself, the transformation is complete. See Nye, *Catalogue*, pp. 1–27, neg. 441361, "GE employees declaring intention to become U.S. citizens in the County Courthouse, Schenectady." The symbolic importance of clothing in Americanization was also evident in the graduation ceremony used by the Ford Motor Company in its Americanization program. See Nye, *Henry Ford*, p. 71.

37. Determined from inspection of graduation lists published each June in *Works News*. Many of these Northern European immigrants were foremen in the plant and thus not strictly speaking the targets of the program.

38. Data from HP-L1466–67. As of January 1923 there were 3,361 foreign-born workers in the Schenectady plant; 45 percent were Italian, 23 percent Polish, with no other immigrant group more than 5 percent.

39. See *Works News*, January 6, 1922, pp. 1–3, January 20, 1922, February 17, 1922, pp. 1–3.

40. Ibid., March 3, 1922, pp. 1, 3.

41. Ronald Schatz, "Union Pioneers: The Founders of Local Unions at General Electric and Westinghouse, 1933–37," *Journal of American History* 66 (December 1979).

42. Lewis Hine, *Men at Work* (1932; New York: Dover, 1976), p. 5.

43. Plate 35, "Americanization Class in Civics, Two Additional Students, 1927," neg. 444217. Also see plates 32 and 33.

Chapter 6

1. Peter L. Berger and Thomas Luckmann, *The Social Construction of Reality* (New York: Doubleday Books, 1966), p. 64.

2. Chandler, *Visible Hand*, pp. 466–467. On the ideology of management, see David A. Wren, *The Evolution of Management Thought* (New York: 1972).

3. Chandler argues that there have only been two basic managerial forms developed in U.S. corporations: "One is the centralized, functional departmentalized type perfected by General Electric and Du Pont. . . . The other is the multidivisional, decentralized structure initially developed at General Motors." This description of General Electric does not square with the data available in the General Electric Archives in the Schenectady plant. Even Chandler's own description would appear self-contradictory; he goes on to state that General Electric's alleged form of organization "has been used primarily by companies producing a single line of goods for one major product or regional market" in contrast to the General Motors form, more suited to "those manufacturing several lines for a number of product and regional markets" (p. 463). General Electric clearly falls into the second category; it served a national market with many product lines and did so from many factories in six different states by 1920. On General Electric's development of a decentralized form or organization, see Ronald Greenwood, *Managerial Decentralization* (Lexington, Mass.: Lexington Books, 1974).

4. Loth, *Swope*, p. 116.

5. Chandler, *Visible Hand*, p. 486.

6. Loth, *Swope*, p. 148.

7. The Association Island phenomenon is not an isolated one. See G. William Domhoff, *Bohemian Grove and Other Retreats: A Study in Ruling Class Cohesiveness* (New York: Harper and Row, 1975).

8. The description of the PYM recruiting system comes from numerous informants inside the corporation who have asked not to be identified. The basic function of these camps is parodied in Kurt Vonnegut's *Player Piano* (New York: Avon Books, 1952), pp. 178–193. His descriptions of the Meadows are based on Association Island.

9. "Camp General, 1930, an Outstanding Event among Association Island meetings," *Monogram* 7, no. 12 (September 1930): 21–22.

10. See "Schedule of Camps at Association Island," *Monogram* 7, no. 7 (April 1930): 32. The camps began July 7 and ended August 30, lasting four days each.

11. *Monogram* 6, no. 11 (August 1929): 3–5.

12. Ibid., p. 3; ibid. 7, no. 12 (September 1930): 30.

13. Ibid., p. 30. See photograph, "March to first tent session meeting at Camp Manufacturing," in Nye, *Catalogue*, pp. 5–8.

14. Loth, *Swope*, p. 149.

15. Lumberjacks in "General Electric management testifying to the cause," neg. 68-C-37. Neg. 68-C-13, "G.E. executives carrying signs, 'We want virgins' and 'Lonesome Eunuchs.' " Men dressed like Roman soldiers, neg. 69-C-25, "Participants in special program at Camp General."

16. Picture of the tree on the cover of *Monogram* 1, no. 2 (1923). Photograph of tree with Light's Golden Jubilee medal on it printed in *Monogram* 6, no. 11 (1929): 4.

17. On the symbolism of trees and poles in other cultures, see Mircea Eliade, *The Sacred and the Profane* (New York: Harcourt Brace, 1968), and his *Patterns in Comparative Religion* (New York: New American Library, 1972).

18. Victor Turner, *The Ritual Process* (Ithaca, N.Y.: Cornell University Press, 1977), p. 96.

19. For an extended discussion of the semiotics of secrecy, see Erik Schwinner, *Power, Silence and Secrecy* (Toronto: Toronto Semiotics Circle, 1980).

20. I refer here to the year when the whole of General Electric began to attend the camps rather than only managers from NELA.

21. "Table of Contents," *Monogram* 1 (November 1923): 2.

22. *Monogram* 1, nos. 1, 4 (October 1923, January 1924).

23. The issues examined were those for February in the even years and for September in the odd years from 1924 until 1929, inclusive.

24. Percentages are only rough indicators since the size of photographs and their placement are more important than sheer numbers. They do not lend themselves to quantification.

25. Industrial landscapes were a staple product of the photography department from the 1890s onward. See Nye, *Catalogue*, chap. 1. Plate 38, "Interior View of Building 85," neg. 324507.

26. Neg. 142950 (plate 39); and neg. 715764 (plate 40).

27. See plate 15, "Portrait of Willis R. Whitney, c. 1910." Compare to plate 41.

28. See, for example, plates 31–35 of Americanization activities.

29. Copley's *Portrait of Paul Revere* reprinted in Barbara Novak, *American Painting in the Nineteenth Century* (New York: Praeger, 1969), p. 24. Colson's *Balthazar Sage* (1777) is discussed in Philip Conisbee's *Painting in Eighteenth Century France* (Oxford: Phaidon Press, 1981), p. 135. Plate 41, neg. 125635. Plates 42–45 (all Steinmetz): neg. 120464, 119886, A83338, A90480, respectively.

30. *Monogram* 1, no. 2 (1923).

31. On the semiotics of tourism, see Dean MacCannell, *The Tourist: A New Theory of the Leisure Class* (New York: Schocken Books, 1976) esp. chaps. 5, 6.

32. For group portraits, see those listed in Nye, *Catalogue*, Chapter V, sections 251–259.

33. Plate 48, "Airplace View," neg. 428194.

Chapter 7

1. One of the better popular works on advertising remains Frank Presbrey's *The History and Development of Advertising* (New York: Doubleday), although published in 1929. His book and an even earlier one by Henry Sampson largely deal with copy: *A History of Advertising from the earliest times* (London: Chatto & Windus, 1874). A detailed study of a single agency is Richard Hower's *The History of an Advertising Agency* (New York, 1887).

2. George Péninou, *Semiotica de la Publicidad* (Barcelona: Editorial Gustavo Gili, 1976; translation of 1972 French edition).

3. Varda Langhol Leymore, *Hidden Myth: Structure and Symbolism in Advertising* (New York: Basic Books, 1975). On butter, baby foods, cheese, and so forth, see pp. 34–56.

4. Chandler, *Visible Hand*, p. 290.

5. Taft, *Photography*, pp. 439–450.

6. Ivins, *Prints*, pp. 150–157.

7. Nye, *Catalogue*, pt. 1, sec. 11–19, 104, contain representative images taken in mines, cotton mills, shoe factories, lumber companies, oil fields, and at the Panama Canal.

8. Chandler, *Visible Hand*, pp. 290–295.

9. Based on knowledge of the archives. See Nye, *Catalogue*, chap. 4, sec. 136. There are few advertising images in the first 100,000 photographs or before about 1905. Paid models, mostly women, make their appearance at this time.

10. Boorstin, *Americans*, pp. 101–112; Chandler, *Visible Hand*, pp. 226–228. Department stores were not only a good place to distribute electrical goods, but they were themselves an excellent customer for electrical elevators, lights, ceiling fans, spotlights, and other forms of electrification. The General Electric photographers shot pictures of John Wannamaker's in Philadelphia, the Jordan Marsh Store in Boston, and many others. See Nye, *Catalogue*, sec. 2, 43, "Interiors of Public Buildings."

11. On developments in lamp business, see Paul W. Keating, *Lamps for a Brighter America* (New York: McGraw-Hill, 1954), pp. 61–72, 75–78.

12. Ibid., pp. 76–77.

13. Mott, *A History*, vol. 4, pp. 3–10.

14. Schuneman, "Photograph in Print," p. 127. The number of photographs per page differed from one type of paper to another. Sunday papers in 1910 had an average of one per page; weekly papers three-quarters of a photograph on average per page. After World War I, when there was a short decline in photography in the newspapers, to one per two pages, use shot up, more than doubling in the 1920s and increasing at a slower pace in the depression.

15. Analysis of magazines based on extensive study of the original documents at Harvard's Widener Library and also confirmed by Theodore Peterson, *Magazines in the Twentieth Century* (Urbana: University of Illinois Press, 1964), p. 21: "Well into the later half of the nineteenth century, however, magazine publishers were almost exclusively purveyors of editorial matter, and many believed that advertising lowered the standing of their publications." He further concurs that advertisements started to move forward only from the "last pages of the magazine to rest between divisions of editorial matter," around 1900. Indeed in 1900, *Harper's* "carried a greater volume of advertising than in the entire preceding twenty-two years combined" (p. 22).

16. Circulations as of 1925: general periodicals such as the *American*, 2.1 million; *Saturday Evening Post*, 2.3 million; *Pictorial Review*, 2.07 million. Scholarly and review periodicals were much smaller: *Harper's*, 67,000; *Century*, 32,000; *New Republic*, 37,000; *Nation*, 33,000; *Scribner's*, 71,000.

17. Keating, *Lamps*, reproduction near p. 64. Also see photograph of Mazda lamp cartons, Nye, *Catalogue*, chap. 4, sec. 132, illustration on p. 4-2.

18. Nye, *Catalogue*, plate 50, "Edison Day Window Display, 1916," neg. 386366.

19. Ibid., p. 4. Two covers reproduced; neg. 385540e. Also see sec. 132 in chap. 4.

20. Photograph reproduced, chap. 4, 4-1, neg. 223801e; similar image on following page, neg. 223713e.

21. Canova's statue is in the Villa Borghese, Rome. David's *Madame Récamier* is at the Louvre, Paris. The General Electric image that copies it has neg. 223713e.

22. José Ortega y Gasset, *The Revolt of the Masses* (London, 1930), p. 89. A series of images shows women producing light bulbs. This series is the only one like it in the General Electric Archives; coming from the earliest period, it appears to be a sequence showing production in its major stages, including packing of the bulbs in boxes. I have not been able to determine why these were taken, or how they were used. Negs. 185459e–185468e.

23. Nye, *Catalogue*, chap. 2, sec. 54 (Fairs and Exhibitions), 55 (World's Fairs), Chicago Electric Show in 1919 depicted in photographs 112382e and 112383e.

24. Ibid., chap. 4, sec. 131. Photograph reproduced from archives, neg. 440969, "G.E. Float in Illinois Central Electrification Pageant, Chicago, August 7, 1926."

25. Plate 57 (electrical kitchen), neg. 204697e; plate 58, neg. 105288.

26. Chandler, *Visible Hand*, pp. 290–292.

27. Hammond, "Psychology," L5141.

28. HP-General Electric Historical File, pamphlet containing advertisements for May to December 1925, "Electricity and the American Public," 1925. Copy also in Widener Library at Harvard. The company did not copyright these materials. See p. 45. Breakdown of magazines by groups on pp. 46–47.

29. Loth, *Swope*, p. 144.

30. For further discussion of this point, see Richard Sennett, *Families Against the City* (New York: Viking Press, 1969), and that more general treatise on family life, Phillipe Ariès, *Centuries of Childhood* (New York: Random House, 1965). I subscribe to the theory that although the extended family may be weakening, the nuclear family has grown stronger and more central to Western culture in the past three hundred years.

31. HP-Pamphlet File, pp. 3–45. Chart developed through analysis of placement of each individual advertisement in magazines.

32. See listings of circulation figures referred to in note 28.

33. Or nearly 20 million subscribers if all of them ran the same advertisement. Most ads went to between eight and twelve magazines.

34. This advertisement was run in *Time, Electrical Worker's Journal, Harper's, Red Book, Wide World, Collier's, Hollands, Magazine of Wall Street, Nautilus,* and *Nation's Business*.

35. Photograph of the Deerfield River automatic hydroelectric plant and accompanying ad appeared in thirteen magazines, including *Nation, Scientific American, Country Life, Popular Mechanics,* and *Outlook*. The Los Angeles substation appeared in eight magazines, including *Collier's, Scribner's, American Legion Weekly,* and *Review of Reviews*. These two lists show that the advertisements were carried in several related groups of periodicals, not targeted for an extremely narrow audience.

36. Ruth Schwartz Cowan, "The 'Industrial Revolution' in the Home: Household Technology and Social Change in the 20th Century," *Technology and Culture* 17 (January 1976): 15. Also see A. Michael McMahon, "An American Courtship: Psychologists and Advertising Theory in the Progressive Era," *American Studies* 13 (1972): 5–18.

37. Cowan," 'Industrial Revolution,' " p. 16. Also see Joann Vanek, "Household Technology and Social Status: Rising Living Standards and Status and Residence Differences in Housework," *Technology and Culture* 19 (July 1978): 361–375. She argues that "in the early decades of the century the media, in particular women's magazines and advertising, proposed a definition of housework that has not changed in substance over the years . . . to combat the glamour and independence of jobs outside the home, the housewife was continually reminded that her work was important . . . a professional job" (p. 367). Basically this was not a new idea, however, having been part of the nurturing ideal proposed to women in the Victorian era; what was new were the psychological dimensions of this role.

38. HP-Pamphlet "Electricity and the American Public," p. 31.

39. All text taken from the advertisement.

40. Jean Baudrillard, *La Société de consommation* (Paris, 1970); Mark Poster,

"Semiology and Critical Theory: From Marx to Baudrillard," *Boundary* 2 (Fall 1979): 281. William Leiss, *The Limits of Satisfaction: an Essay on the Problem of Needs and Commodities* (Toronto: University of Toronto Press, 1976). The same generalizations that Lears offers apply to Roland Barthes's work on advertisements far less than one would perhaps expect. See Barthes's "Rhetoric of the Image," in *Image, Music, Text* (New York: Hill and Wang, 1977), pp. 32–51.

41. Lears's quotation from "The Humbug and the Suckers: Problems and Prospects in the Historiography of American Advertising" (Paper delivered at the Popular Culture Association meeting, Louisville, 1982).

Chapter 8

1. Edward L. Bernays, *Biography of an Idea* (New York, 1965), pp. 456–460.

2. *Books on Municipal Ownership*, Brooklyn Public Library (New York: Brooklyn, 1906). The U.S. Library of Congress also published a bibliography in the same year, "Select List of Books on Municipal Affairs with Special Reference to Municipal Ownership," Washington, D.C., Library of Congress.

3. See, for example, the following, which represents only a very short list: John Burns, "Municipal Ownership a Blessing," *Independent* 60 (February 1906): 449–462; Richard T. Ely, "Municipal Ownership of Natural Monopolies," *North American Review* 172 (March 1901): 445–455. "Fear of Municipal Socialism," *Outlook* 76 (April 1904): 965–968. Louis D. Brandeis, "How Boston Solved the Gas Problem," *Review of Reviews* 36 (November 1907): 594–598.

4. *Utility Corporations* Document 92, United States Senate, 70th Congress, First Session, 1928. Published in 71 parts over seven years. The enormous volume of materials are indexed in Volume 71, and the index alone is more than 530 pages.

5. The summary of the pro public ownership position is drawn from a large number of sources, including those cited in footnote three, and also the following: Charles Whiting Baker, *Monopolies and the People*. (New York: Macmillan, 1899); Frederick C. Howe, *City the Hope of Democracy* (New York: Scribner's & Sons, 1905); and particularly *Annals of the American Academy*, Volume 27, which contains three useful articles, one on Glasgow, another on street railways in Germany, and a third on municipal ownership in Chicago.

6. Richard T. Ely, "Advantages of Public Ownership, and Management of Natural Monopolies," *Cosmopolitan* 30 (March 1901): 557–560.

7. The following paragraph based on these articles: Winthrop M. Daniels, "Municipal Ownership" in Publications of the American Economic Association, 1906, 9: 133–143; Roland Phillips, "Problem of Municipal Ownership," *Harper's Weekly* 51 (September 1907): 1344. "Municipal Socialism," *Quarterly Review* 205 (October 1906): 420–438.

8. See, for example, T. L. Hicks, "Philadelphia Gas Works under Private Operation," *World Today* (October, 1907): 1037; and Ernest E. Williams, "How London Loses by Municipal Ownership," *North American Review* 183 (October 1906): 729–736.

9. See David E. Nye, *Henry Ford: Ignorant Idealist* (Port Washington: Kennikat Press, 1979), pp. 24–26; Ernest Gruening, *The Public Pays: A Study of Power Propaganda.* (New York: Vanguard Press, 1931), pp. 144, 171–173. *Utility Corporations,* op. cit., index lists more than thirty publications issued by NELA and others during the 1920s. See volume 71, 195–198.

10. For a summary of the activities of NELA during the period from 1915 until it came under investigation, see *Utility Corporations, op. cit.,* Document 92, Part 72A, 23–31.

11. Ibid., 28–29; and see Gruening, *The Public,* 131–210.

12. Gruening, op. cit., particularly 174–182. Also see Jack Levin, *Power Ethics* (New York: Alfred A. Knopf, 1931), 112–122, which contains choice quotations from the Senate sponsored hearings.

13. Ibid. (Levin), 123–133.

14. Ibid., 122; Gruening, *The Public,* 178–183.

15. Alan Raucher, op. cit., 75–93.

16. Bouissac, op. cit., Chapter Four, "The Performing Horse," 52–63.

17. See " 'Clever Hans' in a Semiotic Frame," by Thomas A. Sebeok in *Diogenes* 28, 1978. Also, Professor Sebeok discussed the case of Clever Hans at length with the author and in a paper delivered at Union College, March 1981.

18. Compare this communication situation with that for corporate photography described in Chapter Two. This new situation demonstrates the point that while the message may remain the same, the communication does not remain the same when new codes, senders, contexts, and a new contact have been introduced.

19. The Stewart Case was discussed in a paper delivered to the National Convention of the American Political Science Association in December 1928, and later published as *The Challenge of the Power Investigation to American Educators* by Judson King (Washington, D.C.: National Popular Government League, April, 1929), copy in Widener Library.

20. Ibid., 24–25.

21. On NELA educational propaganda, see Levin, op. cit., 70–80 [lower schools], 81–86 [colleges], 94–95 [power conferences], 134–140 [public speaking]. Also Gruening, op. cit., 82–107 [rewriting textbooks], 211–230 [radio, screen, and music], and passim. For further information consult *Utility Corporations Index.*

22. On Swope, see *Utility Corporations,* Part 71-B, 398. On Young, ibid., 438, 545.

23. Ibid., Document 92, Part Three, 14–16.

24. Ibid., Document 92, Part Four, 224–225; 278 ("The 'Romance of Power' is a compilation of slides showing the drudgery of a lot of the people in the world in Europe and Asia.")

25. Gruening, *The Public,* pp. 138–139.

26. *Utility Corporations,* Part Four, 279–280; Part Five 17–19.

27. This generalization most emphatically does not apply to overt public relations, however. See the nine photographic advertisements for private

power reprinted in the 1964 edition of Gruening, *The Public Pays*, between pages xxvii and xxix. One, for example, depicts a baby being spoonfed, his face smeared with baby food, while he smacks his lips. The text begins, "Year-old Alexander Maier of Dayton, Ohio, is one of the newest of the 94 million owners of America's electric light and power companies. . . ." The ad concludes that anyone with a savings account "participates in the profits of the industry." Another ad shows an elderly couple being turned back into East Berlin by armed guards. The text emphasizes that freedom can slip away when the federal government gets too involved in business.

28. *Utility Corporations*, Part Four, 279, contains the only description of the contents of *The Romance of Power* lecture or book. The work itself has entirely disappeared. No copy exists in the Library of Congress, the New York Public Library, Harvard University's Widener Library or even the General Electric Library in Schenectady. The University of Idaho is listed in the Union Catalogue as having a copy, but it could not be located when requested. The sets of slides have also disappeared, but a number of images in the General Electric Archives from c. 1926–1927 appear quite likely as possible candidates for the lecture.

Chapter 9

1. Chandler, *Visible Hand*, p. 433.

2. Erik Barnouw, *Tube of Plenty* (New York: Oxford University Press, 1975), pp. 61–64.

3. On photogravure, see Estelle Jussim, *Visual Communication and the Graphic Arts: Photographic Technologies in the Nineteenth Century* (New York: R. R. Bowker Company, 1974), pp. 56–57, 344.

4. Evans's address to the Royal Photographic Society in 1900 is reprinted in the anthology by Newhall, *History*, pp. 177–184.

5. Walter Benjamin, "The Work of Art in the Age of Mechanical Reproduction," in *Illuminations* (New York: Harcourt, Brace & World, 1968).

6. On the many relations between precisionist painting and photography, see Karen Tsujimoto, *Images of America: Precisionist Painting and Modern Photography* (Seattle: University of Washington Press, 1982), pp. 75–105.

7. On Sheeler, see ibid., pp. 78–82.

8. Nicholas Lemann, *Out of the Forties* (Dallas: Texas Monthly Press, 1983), examines the Stryker project and reproduces many of the photographs.

9. Berger and Luckmann, *Social Construction*, p. 124.

10. On the illegitimacy of biography as a mode of historical understanding, see David E. Nye, *The Invented Self: An Antibiography from Documents of Thomas A. Edison* (Odense, Denmark: Odense University Press, 1983).

Index